A Testament of Faith

D. T. NILES

A Testament of Faith

COMPILED BY
DAYALAN NILES

LONDON
EPWORTH PRESS

© Executors of the late D. T. Niles 1970
First published 1972
by the Epworth Press
All Rights Reserved.
No part of this publication
may be reproduced, stored in a
retrieval system, or
transmitted, in any form or by
any means, electronic, mechanical,
photocopying, recording or
otherwise, without the prior
permission of the Epworth Press,
27 Marylebone Road, London, NW1 5JS
Printed and bound in
Great Britain by
C. Nicholls & Company Ltd

SBN 7162 0180 1

Enquiries should be addressed to
The Distributors
The Methodist Book Room
2 Chester House, Pages Lane
Muswell Hill, London N10 1PZ

Contents

Author's Preface

THIS book is a response to a fourfold pressure. I can almost say that I was ordered to write it.

Can you tell us in some clear sequence what a Christian is supposed to believe?

So many theologians today seem to be able to jettison so much of what was once looked upon as essentials of the Christian faith. Can we follow them?

Can a biblically based faith be articulated today in such a way as to win a hearing?

What is it that is peculiar to the Christian faith which makes the spread of it an obligation?

These questions, however, have not quite determined what this book has become; for, once begun, it took the form simply of a personal testament of faith. There is little argument in it, hardly an attempt to say why I believe what I believe. There is even less disputation in it with those who do not believe as I do, and no controversy at all with other ways of belief. Its only merit is as one man's testimony to the content, nature and power of the Christian faith.

Besides, the method of presentation adopted, leans heavily on the testimony of Scripture itself – not that something is true just because it is stated so in Scripture, but that the way of stating it which is found in Scripture elicits conviction. I only hope and pray that the reader will not find this form of presentation too opaque.

The book is arranged in a weekly sequence, seven units together forming one chapter. The idea was to make the book suitable for daily reading and meditation, and for group study. Last year, I wrote a Lent book on this pattern, devising it as an excursion through doctrine; or perhaps another excursion through Scripture but with doctrine as a primary pre-occupation. To make the journey really worthwhile, it will be necessary to spend time at each place which is visited, and to talk it over with one's fellow-travellers.

Faith today must become obedience tomorrow. The path, though from today or tomorrow is through yesterday. God has acted, and on the record of that action faith must constantly be nourished.

D. T. NILES

Compiler's Preface

THIS is in many ways an incomplete book. My father completed only the first three chapters and got them printed for private circulation as he finished each chapter. The first two chapters were printed in Ceylon and the third chapter was printed in Vellore while he was undergoing treatment.

The first impression we had after his death was that only these three chapters had been done by Papa. But then going through all the papers pertaining to the book given to me by Mama, I discovered that he had practically finished also the fourth chapter. The last two sections of this chapter were incomplete and were written in long hand, but the other sections were typed and ready for printing. I am publishing this chapter as it was found, with also the incomplete last two sections.

The first thing that was given to me after Papa's death by Mama at Vellore was a letter pad on which Papa had jotted down in order the headings of the sections dealing with the Holy Spirit. He had actually indicated the title of the fifth chapter and its subsections and had gone as far as thinking out the title for the sixth chapter. Mama told me that these were the last words he had written and had given this paper to her just before the set back of the last few days.

While arranging his papers in Colombo after I returned from Vellore, I discovered a TWA menu card on which he had jotted down on one side various points connected with the Holy Spirit and on the other side in order the articles of the creed dealing with the Holy Spirit. I have integrated these points into the fifth and sixth chapters that I have written. These chapters are once again very incomplete. They are attempts by me to state my father's teaching. Whenever I have ventured to use my own ideas I have tried to do so in such a way that they would be in agreement with my father's thinking. As you read these chapters you may recall familiar things that were better stated by Papa himself. I take full responsibility for all that is mentioned in these chapters, but at the same time hope that, though inadequate, these will give a glimpse of the lines on which Papa thought about the articles of the creed and the work of the Holy Spirit.

I have been hesitant about writing these chapters. A large part of the credit goes to my wife, without whose encouragement they would never have emerged. I am also thankful to all those who have helped me to finish them. All that my brother and I and our families need say is that Papa and Mama always appreciated whatever we did for them. They rejoiced in our doings and at the same time with helpful criticisms encouraged us to do even better. I have had the courage to write these chapters because I know that they would have appreciated this.

The seventh chapter is once again an incomplete one. I am told that Papa's intention was to write one chapter dealing with general problems of the Christian Faith and this was to be in ten sections. Papa had managed to work fully on only seven sections and these are rough drafts. I am publishing these sections also. They were discovered among other papers at Vallalai.

I hope that the assembling of this book will be appreciated particularly by all those who knew my parents personally and by others who have profited through Papa's preaching and writings.

Methodist Parsonage   DAYALAN NILES
Point Pedro
Ceylon

I believe in God.
Everything is from Him
*   and towards Him and unto Him.*

God is personal.
The personality of each man and woman
*   is derived from and dependent on Him.*

In Him is the meaning
*   which underlies the movement of life*
*   and towards which all life is set.*
God is demand.
To believe in Him is to obey Him.
By faithful obedience to Him is appropriated
*   His gift of wholeness for all life*
*   and all aspects of life.*

God is gathering together a community of faith.
To be made part of that community
*   is to be committed to Him,*
*   to His enterprise with and among men,*
*   and to the way of life which that entails.*

God is Immanuel – God with man.

CHAPTER ONE

I Believe in God

WHY begin with God? Is not God the unknown? Should not the beginning be with what is known and understood? Yes, and yet, when God is arrived at as the end of an argument, it turns out that He is really not God. God is found and known as God or not at all. What I have attempted to do, therefore, is not to seek to prove but to describe: to describe what man and life, nature and history, look like in the light of God. There is no way in which light can be painted except as it is painted by the way its falls.

An artist painting a village street can show it awaking to the morning sun or returning to rest in the evening shadows. The same hillside can be painted in spring or summer, autumn or winter. The light of God too comes with its changes: from dawn to dark, from spring to winter. A testament of faith has to catch this changing light and its varying seasons: depicting it, as best one may, through the pictures that it itself makes possible. God is light.

I Believe

It is generally accepted that, in its earlier versions, the Nicene Creed began – by saying, 'We believe'. The Christian faith is the faith of a community. It is the faith

13

by which a community is constituted, its fellowship nourished, and its vocation determined. The Christian community is not so much a community of believers as it is a community of belief. Within this community the individual is upheld and carried forward as he grows in faith. Faith and doubt come together in various ways in different people. There is no one pattern. But the pilgrimage of the individual is held within and nurtured by the pilgrimage of the community. 'I believe' is a possibility within 'We believe'.

The Christian experience of believing is a complex one. In the first place, and primarily, the Christian comes to believe because he has been grasped by the object of belief – God in Jesus Christ. When a Christian says, 'I believe', he means that he has been turned towards God in Jesus Christ and has been apprehended by Him. The active voice is dependent on the passive voice. I believe because God believes in me. Indeed, it is far more important that men know that God loves them, than that they should be asked whether they love God. It is far more important that men be told that, in spite of everything, God still believes in them; than that they should be asked whether they believe in God. The Gospel is previous to the Creed.

In the Apostles' Creed, there are three paragraphs and each paragraph describes a movement of God. In the first paragraph is described that movement by which God the Father reaches down in creation and providence. The description in the second paragraph is of God the Son as He reaches down in incarnation, suffering and death; and as He ascends again in the events of the resurrection and ascension. The third paragraph describes a movement from down upwards – God the Holy Spirit as He carries humanity up to God, the Church being token and instrument of his movement. It is by this treble movement that men are grasped so that they believe, the content of belief being all the various elements which comprise this action of God. He turns the human mind and will to faith. What He has done and is doing and will do so to turn are what faith is about. Faith is response to God's action. To believe is to know and acknowledge that I am what I am because of Him.

But here is the nub of the believer's predicament that he cannot say 'I am' without saying, 'We are'. This 'we' is a community called together by God and invested with a mission and destiny. The believer believes by his participation in the life of this community. What becomes necessary therefore, is to discern and disclose the relation, within the community of faith, between the experience of the mission of God in and through the Church and the experience of His mission in and to the world. The difficulty of such discernment and disclosure lies in the fact that whereas God's action which faith confesses is a continuous action; its continuity is hidden, as far as the Church is concerned, within its all too human activity and, as far as the world is concerned, within the general secularity of its history. Commitment to the Church's mission, therefore, must go hand in hand with the willingness to accept that that mission, as it is actually conducted, can be different from and in any case is smaller than the total mission in which God is engaged. To put it the other way round, the enterprise to which his faith commits a Christian is larger than the mission of the Church: and because it is larger, his faith equally commits the Christian to help the world to understand the nature of God's mission in it.

Christian belief has an inevitable reference to what are called 'doctrines'. These are the attempts to formulate in propositional language the nature and substance of God's previous actions, the actions previous to faith.

And yet, these doctrines themselves are truly believed in only when they cease to be mere propositions demanding assent, and become rather the means by which faith is sustained and articulated in the midst of the enterprise to which that faith has committed the believer. Indeed, in this context, the doctrines themselves become open-ended and faith becomes an adventure, for there is no way of saying finally what one believes in or of saying exactly what one is committed to, since it is as God's purposes are realised that the meaning of His actions become clearer, and as the mission proceeds that the orders to be obeyed come. One learns as one does.

The act of believing then is directed first of all to a Person, the Person by whom the believer is brought to faith. Secondly, it is directed to an enterprise, the enterprise in which the Person believed in is engaged. And thirdly, it is directed to a particular way of life, a way can be no belief without its consequences in obedience, and the willingness to pay the price of those consequences.

To believe is to affirm the kind of man I want to be. Or to put it differently, when I say 'I believe' I mean that I need to keep on believing. I need constantly to strive for my faith, its integrity and its uncertainty. This is why and this is how individual faith has to rest and does rest on the faith of the community, of all those who have believed and who believe now: the variations of individuals being held within a developing symphony.

Faith and doubt belong together in one indivisible experience. God in Christ who is the object of faith remains beyond demonstrable proof. The enterprise, to which faith commits the believer, remains immersed in the currents of secular history. The way of life, which faith demands, remains an adventure that cannot be set down in a blueprint. It will always be so, until I know even as I am known, until I see and so understand, until He completes in me what He has begun. Until then, and therefore, faith has only one ground – the succour which God provides.

I do believe, succour my unbelief (Mark 9:24).

God

Man, by the very nature of his being suggests a vis-a-vis. He can neither be described or defined by himself. Just as in some forms of music a beat is emphasised by its very absence, so does man point to an absence that asks to be identified. Man is always man-in-relation. The question is, 'In relation to what or whom?'

Man is in relation to the rest of nature. He understands it, cultivates it, controls and cultures it, and enters into rapport with it. In this relation, nature is object to man as subject. Men are also in relation to one another. There is a continuum of human relationship within which are created the continuities of race and nation, class and kindred. Also there is the overall movement of human history within which all life is lived. In this relationship, each man and each group of men are both subject and object to one another.

When God is mentioned as part of the description of man-in-relation, the extra which is asserted in the otherness of God to man. True meeting is always meeting of the other in his otherness: but whereas in every other meeting, the otherness of the object met is qualified by the subject who meets, in the meeting between man and God, it is God who qualifies man.

When the fourth evangelist says, 'No man has ever seen God', he means that no man can ever see God.

17

God can never be object to man as subject. Indeed, in the meeting between God and man, it is man who is the object of God's action.

The word 'God' then is intended to assert a reality in relation to which human life is inevitably lived. The pronoun 'which' however is the wrong pronoun. It suggests that 'God' is simply a particular aspect of human existence. It is when the pronoun 'who' is used that acknowledgement is truly made of God as God, as one who can never be object to man, even though and even when it is man who makes the confession and God who is confessed.

The denial of the existence of God is bound up with and consequent to a particular form of anthropology; an anthropology which seeks to contain man within himself, within the human community, and within nature. Of course, it does not necessarily follow that every denial of God is an actual denial: for many who deny God still assert that life has a meaning and purpose beyond immediate existence, and even beyond the earthly scene. Such assertion, in whatever way it may be made naturally points beyond man: and where there is such a pointer, God is not really denied. Perhaps it were better to say that God is affirmed by denial. A road sign is erected even though there is nothing written on it.

A consistent atheism demands that there be no framework of reference for life as such, no coordinates in terms of which life's graph can be plotted, no norms: so that there is change but no progress, purpose but no goal, right but no wrong. Should however there be smuggled in, into life's description and explanation, the concepts of meaning and purpose, and the distinctions between right and wrong, then the position is no more one of atheism: for man is being affirmed in the dependence of his being on a reality other than and beyond himself.

In the Christian faith, this 'other' is confessed as God, personal in essence and action, and as the source and guarantee of every secondary reality by which human life is sought to be explained. It is these secondary realities which those who seek to deny God usually affirm – the harmony of human society, the creation of a world community, the mutuality of justice, the personal satisfaction of love, the struggle of life to overcome death, and so on. But the nettle which the theist, and particularly the Christian theist, must grasp is this, that God cannot be arrived at as the conclusion of an argument that proceeds from these secondary realities. Rather, for the Christian, these secondary realities become luminous and compelling in the light of God who is affirmed only because He himself has acted, acted in Jesus Christ, and His action has proved self-authenticating.

Man as dependent being, that then is the crucial truth, a truth which is not denied simply because men can act as if they were independent, can choose their relationship with God – whether of acknowledgement or rejection, of obedience or rebellion. The essential fact remains that men have to make this choice. In that God has either to be acknowledged or denied lies the nature of the affirmation implied by the word 'God'. Man's characteristic of dependence is the pointer to the ground of that dependence: his necessity to live by response points to the cause of that necessity.

Logicians argue that it is not permissible to affirm the truth of anything without saying at the same time what it is which, if it happens or does not happen, will prove that the affirmation made is not true. But that precisely is the point about the way in which God is affirmed, that he who affirms God does so always in-spite-of. There is always enough ground to deny that God is.

19

A child affirms the love of its mother. There are many things which can happen or which may not happen which can persuade the child to say, 'I have been wrong. Mother does not really love me.' And yet, not only can the mother's love remain independently true, independent of the child's acknowledgement or understanding: but it can also be that the child's belief in its mother's love is held independently of what happens or does not happen. 'Mother loves' is then not a conclusion but a premise, the premise on which the child depends, the premise on which is founded the child's acceptance of mother. There is a mutual acceptance between mother and child of which the mutuality itself is the ground and guarantee of truth. So it is with God. We accept Him because, in Jesus, He has accepted us.

No one has ever seen God; but God's only Son, he who is nearest to the Father's heart, he has made Him known (John 1:18).

Creation

Christian faith confesses God as Creator. What is being said, however, is not something about when things began, but about their true origin and nature. The doctrine of creation is about the truths concerning the dependent quality of human life and earthly existence. God is first cause only because He is final cause. Creation is not an event in time because time itself is part of creation.

The basic truths in the doctrine of creation are all set forth or implied in the poem on creation with which the Bible opens.

1. Creation means that the universe is not eternal nor self-existent. It is in being because of God. There is a beginning, not in the sense that time began, but in the

sense that God and His creation are separate identities even though inseparably related. God was always Creator. When God created, that was the beginning.

2. This creation is a universe and not a multi-verse. One mind and purpose fashioned it and holds it together. It functions according to laws which are true in the same way everywhere within it. In the midst of all its conflicts, it is amenable to the drive to create unity without uniformity, to create coherence and cohesion without suppressing difference.

3. This is not a completed universe. Creation is dynamic. Constantly chaos gives way to cosmos, order is wrested from disorder, the waste and void yield to life and spirit. Hence the commandment to man that he make fruitful and multiply, that he cultivate and subdue, that he exercise dominion. Hence also the limitation set on man that he may not fulfil his vocation except in the presence of God, a presence which will seek him out of every hiding-place.

4. This is because man alone has been created in the image of God. He lives by reflecting his Creator. And, just as a reflection has no existence in itself, it is neither in the mirror nor in the eye of the viewer, so is God's reflection in man. It is the result of a maintained relationship. Of course, should the mirror be broken, the image will be broken too. Man can and does fragment the image of God which he carries, by letting sin break into and break up his life. And yet the image remains, though as a broken image, for even in his sin God does not leave man alone.

5. Immanuel – God with us – is, therefore, the final fact. It has to be affirmed at every point in the world's tangled story. Not only is nature red in tooth and claw, but human history is strewn with the effects of man's cruelty to fellow man. In the history of thought, there have been many blind alleys and many regressions.

Man's religious life is full of superstitions and marred by fanaticism. The whole story is one of movement through much confusion. This movement, Christian faith affirms, is not a blind one. It is controlled by God's presence and directed to a future which is His intention. At the end we shall be able to say what the Genesis poem says as its climax: 'And God saw everything that He had made and behold it was very good.'

If basic to the being of creation, then, is God's continuing relationship with it, the next question to be answered is: What is the nature of this relationship? The Christian faith affirms a three-fold relation: transcendence, immanence and mutuality.

The affirmation that God is transcendent in an affirmation of God in His otherness. It is imbecile to think that by this 'otherness' a spatial reference is intended. Even the most primitive theology which speaks of God as 'out-there', does not believe that being out-there is part of the nature of Godhead. If God is thought of as 'out-there', it is because man is defined as 'in-here'. Or, to put it differently, the transcendence of God is what sets man on his pilgrimage. Man moves from 'in-here' to 'out-there'. He is no finished product but in process, reaching out to complete rapport with God to whom he is now related but with whom he is not yet at home. And God remains, not what man will eventually become (for God will always be other) but what man will always live by, the power by which he is enabled and the haven to which he arrives.

This means that God is not only transcendent but immanent: that He who is 'other' by the very nature of His being enters into His creation by act of grace. Not only are God's will and purpose embodied in His creation but He himself indwells it. He remains with his creation as the source and strength of its striving and the end and goal of its life. Immanence however is more than 'being-with', it is also 'part-of'. Immanence fulfilled itself in Incarnation. He who was other to man became man. When the Nicene Creed speaks of Jesus as 'begotten not made', this is what it is trying to say. In Jesus, God becomes part of His creation and involved with it in its travel and travail. God is thus both He to whom the human spirit reaches out and He who is the centre of that spirit's inner life.

It is here that is discerned what is meant by the relationship of mutuality. For not only is it true that God dwells in us, but it is also true that we dwell in Him. We live within His life and His life becomes the light within us. The fourth evangelist uses the concept of the Logos to express this truth. As he puts it: 'What God was, the Word was. Through him all things came to be; no single thing was created without him. All that came to be was alive with his life, and that life was the light of men.'

The Word became flesh in Jesus Christ. He was man, man among men: but also the man in whom and through whom men find fellowship with one another and with God. He sustains the mutuality of the God-man relationship. More than the relationship of transcendence and immanence, it is this relationship of mutuality which shows how impossible it is either to evade or avoid God.

God is man's vis-a-vis. He is man's inner truth. He is man's essential predicament.

For in Him we live and move and have our being
(Acts 17:28).

Rule

God's rule maintained through the total story of evolution and the developing history of man is part of the nature of things. God is eternally busy in and with His creation, fashioning it according to His purpose, guiding it to its goal. It is the way in which God is thus busy which is defined by the word 'Almighty'. God remains God even when and even while His purposes struggle for fulfilment. His is the almightiness not of instant power but of all-encompassing rule.

No workman is almighty in relation to the medium with which he works. The carpenter is limited by the nature of the wood, the sculptor by the quality of the marble, the potter by the consistency of the clay. The prophet Jeremiah speaks of God as potter. He decides to make an exquisite pot but finds the clay too recalcitrant. But instead of seeking new clay, He makes the best kind of pot which the clay He has will allow. God does not quench smoking flax but tends it into flame; He does not discard a bruised reed but so notches it as to get out of it the best music of which it is capable.

Of course this is only one half of the truth. The other half is the way in which the clay itself is changed as God graciously works upon it. For God himself is part of the clay. His creating word is embodied in it, His Spirit is at work upon it. Creation goes on because, by impulse within and pressure without, His rule is maintained. His rule is in order that His broken image in each man may come to wholeness, that His whole creation may find its harmony.

The word 'Almighty' has a counter-word which is 'sin': and this word must be looked at. In Christian teaching, there is no attempt to show how sin began or whether it had a beginning. The Genesis story about the fall of man simply seeks to show what sin really is and what its consequences are. The presence of the serpent in the story is an unexplained presence. What the story does is to emphasize the truth that sin is an incursion into human nature and, therefore, also to point to the hope that it will be eradicated. Sin is within God's governance and will finally come to nothing.

For what is sin? It is essentially man's attempt to be man apart from God. To use the Genesis story, there are three elements, which belong to the nature of sin. First, God orders the boundary of human life; but man would rather be free to become as God. Second, God is the arbiter of good and evil; but rather than commit his life to God's will, man would order his own life himself. Third, the natural anxiety which belongs to creaturehood re-inforces man's will to freedom and to responsibility, so setting his foot on a quest for autonomy.

Creation is a climb upward. What the Christian faith affirms is that, at whatever point in this climb upward it is legitimate to speak about 'man', it is essential to speak of him in relation to God. Man is man under God's address. He differs from the rest of creation in that he images God. He has also been invested with the vocation of tending and attention to the rest of creation. And so, because of his borderland situation between God and nature, whatever be the way in which he understands it or acknowledges it, man becomes anxious for his own security, ambitious for his autonomy, and jealous of his authority. To sin is to fall short of the glory of God, that love of God which is so splendid. It is to show oneself too small and too big to be loved by Him, too anxious and too autonomous to find in His love one's peace.

However, sin shall be no more. There is an end. God's rule will come to completion. The triumph of grace will crown the response of faith: and God's love almighty now – unspent, undefeated, unquenchable; will be victorious then – acknowledged, accepted, and enjoyed. Man is a result of his past. He is also the object of a divine purpose and commission. Past and future are together present in every moment of his life. That God's will for man and about man falls athwart

25

man's will for himself is what produces the sin-condition: the condition in which and to overcome which God's rule is maintained.

One further step needs to be taken in speaking of God's rule in relation to the working of sin, and that is to take account of what is called in the gospels 'the evil one'. The core idea in this term is that of the existence of evil outside man. Evil, for instance, can embody itself in social structures which work in terms of their own dynamism. Besides, human beings can and do become channels of evil greater than themselves. There are even times when evil seems to stalk the earth, and occasions when human beings seem to become the abode of evil itself. 'The powers of darkness' is a phrase that allows to evil its own domain. It suggests that sin in man is not all that there is when one is seeking to speak about evil. There is the dimension of the demonic to be reckoned with.

But here again, faith affirms that God rules, the conclusive testimony to the manifestation of that rule being the resurrection of Jesus from the dead. Evil is real, it enacted the cross of Christ. Evil is subject, it could not prevent the resurrection. God's rule does not mean the absence of evil but that it is subject to control, that it is brought to book, and that there are effective processes of reform and renewal. If what God intends is goodness and not conformity, if what He is seeking to create is fellowship and not regimentation, then His almightiness has to express itself in ways congruent with these goals.

To sum up, then, creation is open ended. The universe is not closed. In the midst of sin and evil, God rules: His presence, His patience, and His power bringing to birth a new creation within the old. Old things will pass away and everything become new. And yet, not so simply as it sounds! For patient love, even though almighty, has to suffer its way to victory.

I saw standing in the very middle of the throne, a Lamb with the marks of slaughter upon him (Revelation 5:6).

Kenosis

It has been necessary to say what God's rule means in terms of the condition of the world over which He rules – a world in the making, a creation within which a new creation is being fashioned. What more must be said speaking of Him in terms of His own being and action?

The God who is known is God the Father of our Lord Jesus Christ. Here the determining fact is that in Jesus, God emptied Himself. This action of 'emptying' is part of the eternal nature of God: that quality of His on which are based and on which depend His relation to man and man's relation to Him. The God with whom mankind has to deal is He who has become part of the human situation. God always was and is the Father of Jesus Christ.

When faith is challenged to prove the existence of God, the challenge is usually based on the untenability of believing, with life as it is, that there is a God who is both good and all-powerful. What the Christian faith affirms is that, with life as it is, the only God who makes sense is God as He is in Jesus Christ. He who was Lord lived as servant and at the mercy of those whom He served, so much at their mercy that they could reject Him and kill Him; and yet Lord, whose resurrection they could not prevent.

Since this is a world where evil is at work, where sin has invaded men's lives, where the situation is always a situation in process, a concomitant fact will be the presence of pain and suffering, sorrow and death. In respect of these, God's almightiness, since it is the almightiness of God in Jesus, finds expression in two contradictory ways. There are the ways in which, time and again, the circumstances of life are overcome and the power of the resurrection becomes manifest. And there are the times when men have to continue to live in the shadow of the cross in the strength of the hope of the resurrection, a hope experienced as sufficient grace. God shares the human situation in its sorrow and pain by virtue of His kenosis: He remains sovereign in that situation by virtue of the power which raised Jesus Christ from the dead.

In the Creed, the word 'Almighty' goes with the word 'Father': Father of Jesus Christ, the nature of whose Fatherhood is determined and revealed by the nature of Christ's sonship. God's action of kenosis by which the incarnation took place is what has made possible the knowledge that God is Father. He is Father of Jesus Christ and of those whom Jesus was not ashamed to call His brethren.

What of the time before the incarnation? Is God there apart from His kenosis? By no means. For the kenosis of God was what made creation itself possible, since God tied himself to creation from the beginning. The truth of Immanuel is the truth about creation itself. The biblical concept for conveying this truth is that of 'covenant'. God covenants with man, binding Himself by promises which He will keep irrespective of whether men fulfil their obligations or not.

'I will not destroy you' – that is God's promise to His whole creation. The biblical record uses the story of Noah and the flood to introduce this promise. Not destructive judgement but patience and mercy characterize God's attitude to the world. Indeed, even when judgement arrives, it arrives under the sign of the rainbow. It is not the clouds and the rain but the sun which

is eternal. From God's promise not to destroy flow His actions in judgement and renewal by which the course of history is directed.

'*I will be your God*' – that is God's promise to His chosen people, introduced in the biblical record through the story of Abraham. Here is the basis of His faithfulness to those who know and bear His name. Because of it He chastises them, and because of it He renews them in life and power. The biblical sign of this promise is that of circumcision. Each successive generation belongs to God and is heir to His faithfulness.

If not for His kenosis, and the promises which are the result of that kenosis, God would be pure being who could either be affirmed or denied without any consequence to man. The affirmation 'I believe in God' rests on God's covenant with man, an action of activity of which His kenosis is the heart and substance.

Finally, there is that kenosis of God by which man has been invested with free will. Man is not just the product of yesterday determined in his nature by the past that has produced him. The evolutionary process is also a purposive process. It is by God and reaches out to God. Man's free will is the last gap which has to be bridged before the purpose behind creation is fulfilled. Man has to say 'yes' or 'no' to God's decision about him. He becomes man because God addresses him and claims his response.

Each man's true future is God's will for him, the active presence of this future in each man's life being the constitutive element of his freewill. Conscience, circumstance, one's inner drive and urges – all can be the ways in which that presence is mediated; even though the fulfilment of this presence is in the acknowledged experience of Jesus Christ. The knowledge of the Gospel is God's provision for the true and full exercise of man's freewill.

Creation and freewill, covenant and incarnation – these then determine the perspective from which God's exercise of His sovereignty and almightiness must be discerned. How grievously wrong it would be to seek to trace the footprints of omnipotence in the world and in human lives, forgetting that there would be no footprints at all had not God shed His omnipotence to become the God of His creation.

He knows our frame; He remembers that we are dust (Psalm 103:14).

Pain

Greek thought, to which Christian theology is heir, insisted that God was above pain and suffering. According to it, whenever God entered into the human situation in order to relieve pain or suffering, in order to bring succour to the anxious or distressed, He came from outside. The 'deus ex machina' of Greek drama was a true representation of Greek thought.

The Hebrew conception was more realistic. It perceived the fact that in actual experience there was no 'deus ex machina': and that the God-man relationship was really one of mutual involvement. Pain and suffering, anxiety and distress would always be there, with this difference: that there would be the experience of relief and remission, the experience of succour and courage to bear, the experience of God's presence and power whereby every situation pointed beyond itself to God, in whom was the resolution of and victory over man's present predicament.

In the book of Job, is the picture of a man refusing to accept every form of consolation which his friends seek to bring him in his pain and sorrow. The consolations are too superficial. Job also rejects all the explanations which his friends offer him for his condition. These

explanations are spurious. Ethics, religion, metaphysics
– all are set aside as throwing no real light on Job's
situation. On the other hand, Job seeks an answer from
God himself. He hurls his questions in the face of God,
only to be met by the Divine silence; while in his own
heart he begins to wonder whether he will understand
even if God answers. Can it be that the whole thing is
only make-believe and that the truth is simply that
there is no God? The answer of Job is 'No'. 'I know,'
he says, 'that my Redeemer lives, and that He will stand
upon the earth'. There are no explanations that really
explain. There are no consolations that really console.
There are no answers that come to the questions which
are asked. But God remains. And I know that here and
now, in the midst of my situation whatever it be, I shall
find Him as my Redeemer. 'He will stand upon the
earth.'

How does he stand? What does Immanuel mean,
when God who is affirmed as 'with us' is 'with' because
of His kenosis and only as a result of it? What does it
mean to God that He is man's God? The answer of
Christian faith is in terms of the pain of God. The pain
of God is God's answer to the pain of man, God's true
response to it: and man's response to his own pain is to
make it the pathway by which he enters into the pain of
God. God's pain is the measure of His concern for
His whole creation. It is also the consequences of His
involvement with creation in its struggle with sin and
evil, and in its cry for redemption. Besides, God is not
just Creator: He has also given himself to His creation
in order to be part of it. He is the source of its new birth.

First of all then, God is *concerned with man*. It grieves
Him when men destroy themselves through rebellion or
idolatry. His grief is like the grief of a father whose
son has denied or betrayed the love of his home. His
grief is like the grief of a husband whose wife has be-

31

come a prey of other men. His grief is like the grief of a friend whose friendship has been spurned. There is pain in the heart of God when His purpose for creation is thwarted.

But the pain of God is more than pain on account of man. He is also *involved with man* – involved with him in his struggle with sin, in his contest with evil, in his groping for holiness, in his search for community, in his cry for wholeness. God is a participant in the total movement of life. Indeed, there would be no movement if not for Him. The leaves on the tree would like to be still, but the wind keeps blowing. God engages man and is engaged with man in the pilgrimage of life.

There is more to it even than that. For God suffers also as *part of man*. When there is pain in the human body, it is an indication that the resources of health are resisting and attacking the causes of ill-health. Pain is the symptom which shows that health is actively present. Similarly, it is the active presence of God as part of man which causes both the pain of man and the pain of God. Sin and evil would not cause pain but death were not God actively present.

There is a significant symbolism in the first stories of man in the book of Genesis. Adam is represented as giving to each of God's creatures its name. The rest of creation is subject to men. That is how they become sharers also in man's sinful predicament. God's judgement pronounced on Adam includes the earth also. "In the sweat of your face you shall eat bread". And yet, this very same bread, the sign of men's strife and their toil, becomes in the hands of Jesus the sign of their redemption. "This is my body broken for you." The symbol of man's pain becomes the symbol of the pain of God. The one bread becomes the symbol of the double pain.

The judgement pronounced on Eve was that in pain

and travail she would bring forth children. The pain of child-birth is used to symbolise the pain in which all life is involved. The generations succeed one another in pain. But this very pain of child-birth becomes the symbol of God's travail for His new creation. 'I travail in pain', says St Paul, 'until Christ be formed in you'. 'The whole creation travails,' he says, 'waiting for its redemption.' The words of Jesus to Nicodemus, 'You must be born again', have become Christian common-place. What is forgotten is that it is the mother who must give birth to her child. God is the mother of the new birth. No man can make himself to be born again. And birth involves pain – for the mother!

He shall see the fruit of the travail of his soul and be satisfied (Isaiah 53 : 11).

Glory

It should now be evident that when a Christian says, 'I believe in God', he is declaring his response to God in His action and activity: an action and activity which concern the whole created universe and all mankind, and concern also each person in such a way as both to demand and to evoke the response of obedient faith.

The central action of God which is celebrated in the Old Testament is the creation of a people who will serve His purposes, witness to His Name, and be a sign of His will for all mankind. The call of Abraham, the exodus from Egypt, the settlement in Canaan, the foundation of the Kingdom of David, destruction at the hands of Assyria, exile in the land of Babylon, the return to Jerusalem, the restoration of city and temple – all belong together as one story declaring who revealed His name to Moses as 'I am that I am' – 'I am what I shall be'. He is dynamic constancy, purposeful activity, His every action holding within it also future promise.

33

The central action of God celebrated in the New Testament too is the creation of a peculiar people. But whereas in the Old Testament, the story is the story of the people themselves, in the New it is the story of a person. The birth of Jesus and His ministry, His passion and his death, His resurrection and ascension – that is the decisive event. In it the old is re-constituted, and a new brought into being. He becomes for both the foundation of their history and the on-going reality of their lives.

The event, however, is not yet over. Indeed, whether in the New or in the Old, the event is such that it not only evokes the affirmation of faith but also the expectation of hope. The story of Israel constantly and consistently pointed beyond itself to the purpose of God for all mankind, giving rise to the hope of the Messiah. In Jesus, the Messiah came. But the action of God in Jesus is not completed either. Jesus will return to complete what He has begun.

The Christian faith confesses God as 'Him who is and was and is to come'. It is not accidental that the third phrase does not say "who is to be". The affirmation made is not that God is in the process of becoming. God is God, eternally so. 'He is the same yesterday, today and for ever': unchangingly constant amidst ongoing purpose. However, since the eternal God has a purpose in time and for time, He himself has entered into time and will bring time to its completion. He is known and confessed through His self-disclosure involved in this activity.

The word in the Bible which is used to convey this quality of God is the word 'glory'. His glory becomes manifest through His activity, and it is to His glory that men make response. Everything that belongs to God is splendid. His purposes are all encompassing. He is faithful to the last limit. The glory of God is the glory of His love; so constant, so inexhaustible and so trust-worthy. To confess this glory and to live by it is to glorify Him.

In the New Testament, the word 'glory' takes on a deeper level of meaning. There is the glory of God as it becomes manifest in His kenosis and through His pain. The glory of God is the splendour of God's love poured out. This is why it is right to speak of Jesus as having been glorified on the cross. The mandate of the Church is to bear testimony to this glory. It lives by sharing in that cross; sharing in it as the source of its own life and the means of fulfilling its mission.

By the very nature of God's self-disclosure, therefore, the act of faith includes an attitude of hope. To believe in God is also to hope in Him. An essential part of the response to what God has done is that firm expectation of what God will do: so that obedience in order to serve the purposes of God which lie in the future becomes an integral part of the Christian life.

Emphasis on the future as part of one's confession of God, however, must not lead to the misunderstanding that God is himself subject to process. God is God, and kenosis is by His own free will. It is by His own decision that He has involved himself in the evolution of His creation and the redemption of man.

Himself not subject to process, God has yet by deci-sion of grace involved himself in the world. His pain is real pain. But whereas human pain carries with it the connotation of sin, 'God is light and in Him is no dark-ness at all'. He remains gloriously God in the midst of His involvement with men. His patient faithfulness to a faithless people was His glory. Christ's willingness to die a felon's death was that glory's culmination.

God's glory, however, is not simply that glory from which kenosis proceeds, nor the glory of the kenosis itself: it is also the glory which is the outcome of the kenosis – the glory seen in Christ's resurrection. Towards this glory the Christian hope is set, and by this hope Christian obedience is sustained. The future is a guaranteed future: guaranteed by the resurrection. The glory made manifest there will fulfil its promise. He will come again.

The Christian has to live his life at the foot of the cross. There he will taste of the glory that belongs to the experience of sin forgiven, of sorrow borne, of sickness endured. But sometimes he will know also the glory of the resurrection, of sin conquered as well as borne, of sickness healed as well as endured. Today is never the unqualified context of Christian living. Yesterday and tomorrow will always be part of the existential situation. The Gospel and the Eschata are part of today.

The Lord is my portion, therefore I will hope in Him
(Lamenations 3 : 24).

God is One.
The Father of Jesus Christ is the one God.

He is known
　　through His self-disclosure in Jesus Christ,
　　and in the history of the people
　　of whom Jesus Christ was.

God, the Father of Jesus Christ
　　is also the Father of all men,
His providence is equally for all.

In Him, humanity is one,
　　and by Him,
　　the several histories of persons and communities
　　are brought together to become one history.

There is one judgement, one mercy;
　　one mission, one destiny;
so that all creation which is from Him
is also through Him and unto Him.

The Christian community exists within the human
　　　　　　　　　　　　　　　　community,
　　making visible the hidden purposes of God's
　　　　　　　　　　　　　　　　working,
　　making vocal the silent mystery of God's grace,
－　and making credible God's intention to redeem
　　all men and all things in Jesus Christ.

CHAPTER TWO

God is One

THIS chapter has got itself written in a way that I had not anticipated or intended. I simply wanted to express the belief that God is One and that there is only one God. I find that what I have done is to show what such belief entails. Besides, whereas I had expected to rest the exposition of this belief on general grounds, I found that it actually did not rest on general grounds in a way that could be expressed generally. The foundations are in the faith and exprience of the community of faith as these are attested to in Holy Scripture.

Naturally, such writing as this will not carry conviction to those who stand outside the tradition, but it will at least make that tradition understandable. The movement from understanding to faith is necessarily a mystery. Faith is the result of having been made captive by Him towards whom that faith is addressed.

The movement of thought, reflection and conviction by which man comes to say, 'I believe in God' is matched by a complementary movement which leads him to affirm that 'God is One'. Indeed, God is not confessed as God until His universality and unity are part of that confession.

As one reflects on the long pilgrimage of the human mind and spirit, one discerns in it a three-fold progression. First of all, there is the journey from magic to science, and through science to technology. The whole is seen as a whole, as a *uni*verse – a causal unity, dependable and predictable, and therefore controllable. Control is exercised in order that the universe may serve human ends. Secondly, there is the journey from taboo to ethics, as a consequence of which life-together finds its foundation in relationships of mutual obligation, whose authority is other than man and his immediate desires or needs. The moral discovery is concomitant with the discovery that true life is life in community. Thirdly, there is the journey from animism to some form of theism (or atheism), by which man's true relation to his vis-a-vis is affirmed as one of responsibility and accountability. The universe and human life within it are seen as subject to and implicated in an all-controlling purpose, with the consequence that all life and all things are knit together not only by common natural laws, not only by mutual moral obligations, but also by an all-encompassing destiny. Life and living are acknowledged as having a destination; by which, therefore, each life is judged and regulated, vindicated or destroyed.

Where the paths of these three journey's intersect, there God is confessed. God is One, the God of all and therefore the God of each, in whom all causal laws inhere, from whom all moral obligations proceed, by whom all histories are made part of one history.

In primitive societies, belief in an over-all spirit presiding over a spirit-world was quite common. But this over-all spirit was not the object of faith or of worship. Warring peoples could not worship the same god. Each warring group, race or nation, therefore, had its own god. The gods themselves went to war. At the stage of settled community life, there were recognized presiding deities over various territories. The contest of Elijah on Mount Carmel was a contest to prove the impotence of the Baal in the territory and among the people who belonged to Yahweh. At a later stage was the problem which the early prophets of Israel faced with their people. This was the wish of the people to worship both Yahweh whose function was as the God of war and the Baalim who were conceived as the gods of agriculture. A different concept of plurality is that found in Vaishnavite Hinduism, for example, in which the various Avatars are explained as the coming into the world from time to time of the one God in order to establish righteousness and punish wickedness.

What is the road from plurality to unity?

In the history of religion, there have been two distinct and contrasted ways in which the ultimate universality and unity of God have been affirmed over against the plurality of the gods. One way was to allow that there was partial or contingent validity in every confession of 'god', and to say that behind and beyond the 'gods' there was God of whom or of which these were so many manifestations. Or, to put it differently, there were many imperfect human acknowledgements of the one God. When the universality and the unity of God are postulated in this way, God usually remains the unknown and the unknowable, spoken of with equal validity in the masculine or the neuter. The eternal Dharma, the ineffable Tao, the unqualified Brahman, the ultimate Wisdom – all become the symbols in human language of Him or of That of whom to speak is always to distort.

But when a Christian says, 'God is One', he is speaking out of a different religious history. Abraham builds altars to God under every green tree, even as the Canaanites did for their Baal. Later, Yahweh, as Israel confessed Him, takes His place alongside other gods: Dagon of the Philistines, Moloch of the Ammonites, Melkaart of the Phoenicians. The early prophets contended for the loyalty of Israel to Yahweh alone. The first commandment enjoins this loyalty. 'I am the Lord your God, who brought you out of the land of Egypt. You shall have no other gods before me.' However, they do not deny the other gods.

It was not till very much later that there dawned in Israel's religious history the conviction that Yahweh could not be God, were He not also the only God. And, He could not be the only God, if His attitude and concern for others were not equal to His attitude and concern for Israel. 'God,' says Amos, 'brought Israel from Egypt' – that was Israel's religious watershed. 'But He also brought the Philistines from Caphtor and the Syrians from Kir.' The Philistines and Syrians were Israel's hereditary enemies. Yahweh was their God too, *and in the same way.* 'Turn to me and be saved, *all the ends of the earth!* For I am God, and there is no other.'

God is One and He is known. He is not the unknown and unknowable. He is the Lord, Yahweh. He is the God of *our* fathers. Now, however, we see that He is also the God of *their* fathers. The gods whom they actually worshipped were not gods at all. God was their God nevertheless, their God all the time. Now, He demands of them that they turn to Him, so that in true response and humble obedience they may find and fill their place in His economy. 'The times of ignorance God overlooks.'

This history of thought and discovery is basic to the Christian confession that God is One: for what is affirmed is not simply that there is one God, a unity behind and beyond all plurality: but that this God, known and acknowledged and obeyed, is indeed the God of all and the God of each – one God by whom the pluralities are judged and left behind.

There is one God, the Father, from whom all being

41

comes, towards whom we move; and there is one Lord, Jesus Christ, through whom all things came to be, and we through Him (1 Cor 8:6).

One Providence

There is in the hundredth psalm a call to the peoples of all lands to worship the one God. This God, the psalmist says, is the Lord, the God whom Israel worships. To the question, 'How do you know?' he gives the surprising answer – 'The Lord is good'.

If there was one thing to which Israel could bear witness, it was to the goodness of God: a goodness so unwearied and unfailing that it had followed Israel throughout its long history and indeed fashioned that history. God had been faithful to His people in spite of every unfaithfulness on their part. He had not rejected them when they had rebelled against Him. He had not discharged them from their mission even when they showed no interest in it. He punished them, He forgave them, He recalled them to obedience and continued to trust them with His purposes. As at the burning bush where Moses had his vision, so Israel had come to know God as a goodness that was never consumed even though it was always on fire.

This goodness, the psalmist now claims, is God's attitude to all men, to every people, to each nation. He is their good God as well.

In the opening sermon of Jesus at Nazareth, He reminds His hearers of two incidents in their history. During the famine in the time of Elijah, God sent His prophet to relieve the distress of a widow who was a Sidonian. She did not know or worship Yahweh. There were many lepers in Israel during the time of Elisha, but God used Elisha to cure the leprosy of a Syrian. This direct reference to God's goodness shown to the hereditary enemies of Israel was what riled the congregation at Nazareth.

The passage of scripture which Jesus read when He spoke at Nazareth was a passage concerning the mission of the Servant of the Lord. According to this passage, the objects of the Servant's ministry are not any particular people, people of any particular religion or race. God comes to meet human need wherever it is found: the blind, the lame, the poor. It is said of the same Servant – 'All we like sheep have gone astray; and the Lord has laid on Him the iniquity of us all.' The ultimate need of men for forgiveness is met without any questions being asked of who they are. All are included.

The prophet of the Old Testament who wrote these songs of the Servant gives expression to the universalism of God's providence by going even further. He takes the case of Cyrus, King of Persia, and says that not only is God's graciousness to other peoples than Israel demonstrated by the way in which God called and anointed and used him; but that he is also an example of the way in which God's graciousness to Israel is shown through other people. God says to Cyrus: 'I am the Lord, and there is no other; I gird you, though you do not know me.'

This universalism is implicit even in the early stories of the Old Testament. The characters of those stories come in pairs – Cain and Abel, Lot and Abraham, Ishmael and Isaac, Esau and Jacob – and the point of each story is the way in which God is with each person in each pair. Abel, Abraham, Isaac, Jacob – that is the lineage of God's mission. They are the bearers of history. But God's providence is also for Cain, for Lot, for Ishmael and for Esau. God's mark is set on the forehead of Cain, Lot is delivered from destruction, God promises to be with Ishmael also, Esau is made the father of a great people.

The Christian's faith is in an equal providence though not in a similar providence for all. Then Amos says to Israel on behalf of God, 'You only have I known of all the families of the earth; therefore I will punish you for all your iniquities', he is stating a consequence of what God's providence can mean to those who are the bearers of God's mission. When St Paul says, 'God's grace is sufficient for me,' he is speaking primarily of his experience as a missionary. Through every vicissitude in life, St Paul experienced the providence of God as sufficient to enable him to fulfil his task and his vocation.

This is one side. The other side is the providence of God as it is experienced by everybody. Jesus puts this truth in a very simple form when He says that God makes the sun rise on the evil and the good and sends rain on the just and the unjust. No questions are asked. The Father knows, the Father remembers, the Father cares – not one sparrow is forgotten. 'Be not anxious, therefore', was the teaching of Jesus. He warned men against many kinds of sins but concerning none was He more emphatic than the sin of anxiety. To be anxious was to forget the Father.

In the Christian faith, the providence of God has also a third aspect: it is an expression of God's concern for life's final destiny. When, in his letter to the Romans, St Paul says, 'In everything the Spirit co-operates for good with those who love God and are called according to His purpose'; he is speaking about that Good which he has already defined. The good to which all things contribute is the experience of sonship to which all persons are called. This is each man's final destiny. God's providence cannot, therefore, be at any time exclusively in terms of a person's immediate needs. We are always on the way to our destination and providence is for the journey.

44

Life is such that, again and again, the question will arise as to why something happened, what God intended or intends through a particular experience, how one may live in faith in the midst of inexplicable circumstance. The mystery of providence which this questioning seeks to probe can never be completely resolved. But such answer, as it is possible to find, will lie at the point where God's threefold concern is equally grasped. *He whom God has enlisted in His mission must be maintained in His vocation. Every child must be cared and provided for. Each must be helped along the journey to his final destination.*

Once God has spoken, twice have I heard this; that power belongs to God; and that to Thee, O Lord, belongs steadfast love (Psalm 62:11-12).

One History

The natural consequence of one providence is one history. Everything and everybody are held within one meaning. God's purpose for each finds its fulfilment in God's purpose for all. The belief that God is one must make impossible any conception of life understood simply in terms of individual fulfilment.

The Christian word for man's final destiny is 'salvation'. Salvation is the restoration of each to wholeness and the restoration of all into a whole. God's purpose, says St. Paul, is that 'the universe, all in heaven and on earth, might be brought into a unity in Christ'. Within this purpose, God's purpose for each is 'mature manhood measured by nothing less than the full stature of Christ'.

In the book of Genesis, human history is represented as worked out under three signs. The first sign is that of the flaming sword at the gate of the Garden of Eden,

45

from which man and woman have been driven away. They have gone out claiming as their responsibility the right to decide between good and evil. They will live as they decide. The flaming sword stands as the symbol of the mortality and finitude of this life. Before man can inherit eternal life, he has to subject himself to God's judgement. He has to accept that it is God who has the right to decide what is good and what is evil. The God of all alone can be the God of each.

Nevertheless, man's life lived within the context of finitude and mortality is also lived within the context of God's mercy. The second symbol under which human history is worked out is the symbol of the rainbow. The rainbow is proof that the sun is shining even when it cannot be seen. Rain and storm are the conditions of human life, but a rainbow is arched above them testifying to God's presence with man in mercy and faithfulness. *We cannot know God as He is, we only know Him as He is with us.* The description we have in the Bible is not of the sun but of the rainbow. It is a description of the ways in which God remains and shows Himself to be man's God.

The third symbol is that of the unfinished tower. Those who sought to build a tower reaching up to heaven were seeking a way of making God subject to the human predicament. They wanted a tower so high that another flood would not be able to submerge man without also submerging God. This project came to nothing. 'God with man' does not mean that God ceases to be God. God can never be made just a quality or dimension of human life.

St Paul brings these truths together into a compelling confession when he says: 'It is not because God lacks anything that He accepts service at men's hands, for He is himself the universal giver of life and breath and all else. He created every race of men of one stock, to inhabit the whole earth's surface. He fixed the epochs of their history and the limits of their territory. They were to seek God, and, it might be, touch and find Him.'

God accepts service at men's hands – history has a meaning. *He created every race of men of one stock* – history is one. *He fixed the epochs of their history* – history is not autonomous. *They were to seek God* – the history of each person is determined by this search.

Three strands have already been distinguished as being woven together into one movement. The first strand is that of personal history. The story essentially is of how men come to live by faith in God. The experience of faith is the experience of stretching one's hand into the dark and finding that it is held. A man launches out outside himself and finds that his adventure has been charted for him. This is why, whereas a description of how man finds God must start from the human end, the description of what he finds has to be given in terms of what God himself discloses when He is found. Indeed, God's self-disclosure is not simply at the end of a human finding. It is itself an invasion of man by God. Men find themselves caught and held, a conviction that was not there suddenly comes to be there. God's presence becomes a presence that cannot be denied or evaded. Faith is born and one does not know how it has happened.

But all these personal histories of finding and being found do not stand alone. They work into a larger history in which the story is that of communities and nations. This is the second strand. Secular history is also in God in Jesus Christ. Men in community have to find ways of obedience to Him even though and even when they do not know that it is Him whom they obey. With every new invention, by which transport and communication become easier and faster, the world shrinks. Today, as never before, the whole world is a neighbourhood. Men are faced with the choice of learning to live together or of destroying one another. The wholeness of community-life has become an inescapable responsibility. This challenge too is part of man's history under God.

In the story of the Church, which is the third strand, are the token and instrument of this double movement towards wholeness. The Church is the bearer of the gospel of God in Jesus Christ: the news of God and man made one. The Church lives by making this news known and effective in human lives. It also lives by demonstrating the possibility of human community across every division – a calling so often betrayed! For while the unity of the Church is indeed given by its Lord on its members lies the responsibility 'to make fast with bonds of peace the unity which the Spirit gives.' The Church fails the world when it fails to give evidence of its community life in Jesus Christ.

In the vocation of the Church faithfully fulfilled takes place the surfacing of that undercurrent by which the direction of all things is set.

In Christ indeed we have been given our share in the heritage, as was decreed in His design whose purpose is everywhere at work (Ephesians 1:11).

One Mission

There is one providence by which all life is lived and each life is upheld. There is one history within which all histories are knit together. There is one mission of God in the world which is the inner stream of this one history. What is this mission? The Johannine declaration runs like this. 'God loved the world so much that He gave His only Son, that every one who has faith in Him may not die but have eternal life. It was not to judge the world that God sent His Son into the world, but that through Him the world might be saved.'

God loved the world – *that is the scope of the mission.* By the word 'world' is described life in the complexity of all its relationships. God loved men in their life together. The world is not just individuals, one by one. God sent His son – *this was how the mission was launched.* The method of God's mission in and to the world was to become part of it. The 'with-ness' of God took human form. In Jesus Christ, God lived a human life. This life did not end with death but continues, because Jesus Christ rose from the dead. It is this life which is eternal – beyond time, even though lived in time. That men share in this eternity is what God intends. *That is the purpose of His mission.* To die or to perish is to become useless. When a fruit has perished, it has to be thrown away. When a tree has died, it has to be cut down. To live in Christ is to become useful to Him in His mission, in His work of salvation. Salvation is received precisely when it is shared.

The life which Jesus lives inevitably brings all life to judgement: and yet that is not His purpose. His purpose is salvation, the restoration to wholeness.

Wherever, then, life in any of its aspects is being restored to wholeness, whatever and whenever aspects of life which have flown apart are brought together again, there the mission of God in Jesus is finding fulfilment. The enrichment of life depends upon differences: between human life and the rest of nature, between man and woman, between age and youth, between race and race, nation and nation, culture and culture, religion and religion. These differences constantly tend to break out in conflict. They have to be reconciled. And yet, no particular reconciliation is ever permanent. As the potential of each increases with the advance of knowledge, new reconciliations have to be effected at deeper and deeper levels. The work of salvation is never a finished work. Why! even in the case of an individual who comes to faith in Jesus, it is never possible to say: 'Now that is done. He is permanently saved.'

In this work of salvation, Christ, uses many instruments. He uses individuals who confess and belong to Him. He uses the Church which is the company of those who bear His name. He uses many who do not know Him, but whose obedience is to the light as they have seen it. There is no true enlightenment apart from Him. He even uses, to use St Paul's phrase, 'the vessels of wrath made for destruction'.

This mission of God in Jesus Christ constitutes the insistent pressure behind every movement of human history. The dialectic of history is not just an immanent dialectic. It is subject to a compelling purpose so that, in the long view, history is not just the story of man but the story of God *with* man and man *with* God.

Jesus is the missionary and His is the mission. As the writer of the epistle to the Hebrews puts it, 'He is the Apostle and High Priest of the religion we profess'. The word 'apostle' means missionary. To be High Priest means that the mission is now mediated. While the mission as Christ conducts it, can draw into its service any whom He wills to use, there is nevertheless that point at which the mission becomes visible and vocal. A missionary community has been created to be the task force on which the mission depends.

What is the mandate of this community? St Matthew's gospel closes its narrative with the setting forth of this mandate. Jesus says to His disciples, 'Full authority in heaven and on earth has been committed to me. Go forth therefore . . .' Their mission is the consequence of His authority. Indeed, their mission is part of the way in which He has chosen to exercise His authority. They go to make that authority acknowledged and obeyed.

This means, in the first place, the task of discipling the nations. The word 'nation' in the Bible means any grouping that lives a common life. A tribe is a nation. Those engaged in the same enterprise are a nation. A college community is a nation. The Christian mission seeks to bring these several ways of common life into discipleship to God's will for them in Jesus Christ. Man being God's creation through Christ made in God's image, his humanity is God's will for him. To disciple the nations is to lead them into a fulfilment of this humanity. Here is the engagement of the mission in secular history.

The second part of the mandate is that men be baptised everywhere in the name of the Father and the Son and the Holy Spirit. (The Trinitarian formula was the actual formula used at the time St Matthew's gospel was written). Here is set forth that aspect of the mission which shows its involvement in the personal history of individuals and in the building up of the Church.

Then follows the command, 'Teach them to observe all that I have commanded you.' The mission is to be carried on from generation to generation. Obedience to Him is never a completed objective. The history of man and God's mission within it remain a continuing movement. And so the mandate ends: 'Be assured I am with you always to the end of time.'

So we who have found safety with Him are greatly encouraged to hold firmly to the hope that is placed before us (Hebrews 6:18).

One Humanity

In the pages of the New Testament, one reads of the ways in which the first Christian community sought to establish wholeness of relationship between male and female, husband and wife, parents and children, masters and servants, believer and unbeliever, government and subject, slave and free. The task of reconciliation in all these areas of life still goes on. But there was one battle that was fought to a finish within the first years of the Christian mission: a battle through which emerged the conviction that all mankind was one. Apart from this conviction there could have been no real dedication to the several tasks which the Christian mission implied.

The one big cleavage between man and man which the early Church had to deal with was the cleavage between Jew and Gentile. Here was a cleavage rooted in the very history of the faith. God had chosen Abraham. He had preferred Jacob to Esau. What then was the relation in Christ between Jew and Gentile? The natural answer was somehow to keep the Church within the categories of Jewry and to find room for the Gentiles in the Church within this category.

God led the Church by another road. When one reads the story of how God did this, one is surprised by the simplicity of the action. Philip, the evangelist, is walking along the road from Jerusalem to Gaza. An Ethiopian going along the way gives him a life in his chariot. He talks to the Ethiopian about Jesus Christ. The Ethiopian finds faith and asks for baptism. There is no one there whom Philip can consult. There is no precedent for Philip to follow. The Ethiopian is baptized, even though he was not circumcised. Peter is led to the house of a Roman. As Peter preaches, Cornelius and his household receive the Holy Spirit. How can

Peter refuse them the baptism of water when the Holy Spirit had already baptized them? Paul is led by his zeal for the Jewish law to persecute the Christians. He discovers the love of Christ for him, the persecutor. That love makes him whole in a way in which his obedience to the Law never made him whole before.

St Paul puts the matter directly. 'Christ Jesus is Himself our peace,' he says, 'Gentiles and Jews, He has made the two one ... so as to create out of the two a single new humanity in himself.'

This fact of one humanity has many consequences. Its most far-reaching consequence is to make the human itself the standard of judgement. Basic to the movement of history and central to the mission of the Church is the cry to make human life in all its aspects more human. Indeed, it would not be wrong to say that even when an individual or a group have become Christian in their allegiance, they may, and often do, need to go a long way still before they attain human-ness. Their conditions of life may not yet be human, or they themselves may not be sufficiently human in their relationships to one another or to their fellow men.

By the same token, every form of allegiance – whether religious, communal, cultural, national or racial – is subordinate to the demand of the human. There is no way by which the humanity of another may be validly denied or denigrated. It cannot be done on the ground that he does not accept a particular creed or allegiance or loyalty or political system. The situation is worse where the condition laid down for the full acceptance of another's humanity is that he would belong to a particular race or colour or caste.

Once the oneness of humanity is affirmed, it is then possible to affirm the differences within the one humanity. The differences become a source of enrichment and not of division. For instance, there is no unity worth speaking about were one speaking just about a plain piece of cloth. On the other hand, the unity of a tapestry is a true unity. Unity is a dynamic fact. Differences of colour and shape and form come together to produce a unit. The process of human-ness involves the creation of this kind of unity. The one humanity in Christ is a multi-coloured reality.

But just as the one humanity embraces diversity; even so, it also provides the condition under which each separate element becomes human and retains its human-ness. Isolation is an inhuman method of life, whether the isolation be adopted or enforced. It is part of the process of history that every attempt at isolation finally comes to nothing. The one humanity is the truth which brings to nought every attempt, overt or covert, to deny it.

This one humanity, however, is not just an idea or an ideal. It is possible to point to it. It is built 'upon the foundation laid by the apostles and prophets, Christ Jesus himself being the foundation stone. In Him the whole building is bonded together'. The human community and the Christian community belong together and to one another. 'The mustard seed', said Jesus, 'was one of the smallest of seeds. But when it grew it became a tree in which the birds of the air would build their nests.' However insignificant the carpenter of Nazareth was, He would increase, and all humanity would find in Him its abiding place. But the 'increase' – that is the necessary pre-condition: a pre-condition whose fulfilment can neither be dissociated from nor identified with the increase of the Church.

The distinctiveness of the Christian community within the human community lies simply in its relation to the mission of Christ; for while that mission is certainly more than the Church's mission, it is still the heritage of the Church in a way in which it is the heri-

54

tage of no one else. To be saved as individual men and women is to enter into this heritage, to accept responsibility for it, and to live out of it. Ultimately, salvation is not what each receives but all enter into. For God's gift of salvation is the gift of Christ himself.

For there is one God, and also one mediator between God and men, Christ Jesus, himself man, who sacrificed himself to win freedom for all mankind (1 Timothy 2:5–6)

One Judgement

The mystery of a missionary community within the one humanity comes to its most forceful expression in what the Bible has to teach about the nature of God's judgement. It has to be so, because if salvation is God's gift offered to all, it must necessarily become also the basis on which all will be judged.

When Amos opens his book of prophecy, he opens it with a declaration of the Lord as Judge of all the nations. Whether they acknowledge Him as Lord or not, He is their Lord, and it is by Him that they will be judged. In the indictment which he makes against the nations, he accuses them of cruelty and inhuman-ness. The accusation stands whether the wrong done is done to Israel or to Israel's enemy. Ammon is to be punished because of what it did to Israel, but Moab is to be punished for what it did to Edom. Edom was Israel's inveterate enemy. When Amos comes to accuse Israel itself, the basis of his indictment, however, is the vocation of Israel and its faithlessness to that vocation. There is one Lord and one judgement, but that judgement is as complex as the complexity of history.

According to the prophet Isaiah, Sennacherib the Assyrian is the rod of Yahweh's anger against Israel. The prophet of the exile speaks of Cyrus the Persian as the anointed of God and His servant. St Paul speaks of Pharoah of Egypt as having been raised up by God 'for the purpose of exhibiting God's power, that God's fame may be spread over all the world'.

All belong to the one humanity over whom God exercises judgement with impartiality: an impartiality, however, which does not mean either that all are judged by the same standards or are punished in the same way. God's judgement is always related to the movement of history – be it the history of the individual or of secular society or of the Church. That which is judged remains within the movement within which it is enmeshed.

When Jesus talks about God's judgement, His main emphasis is that judgement takes place simply because of the un-evadable presence of God. The fourth evangelist puts it thus, 'All that came to be was alive with His life, and that life was the light of men'. 'But men preferred darkness to the light because their deeds were evil.' The light is never of the same brilliance to every man or in every situation. Nevertheless, it is light; and men judge themselves and are judged by it. They decide for themselves whether they should hide or not. There are differences of judgement, even though the presence by which the judgement is effected is the same.

In the parables of Jesus, such as that of the talents and that of the husbandmen, the divine presence is represented as a call for an accounting. This call will always come. The servants have to say what they have done with the money entrusted to them. The husbandmen must pay that which is due to the owner. There is no way of saying, 'I do not need to render an account. My life is mine.' In the parable of Jesus about the sheep and the goats, the divine presence takes another form, the form of the marginal person in society – the hungry, the thirsty, the naked, the prisoner, the stranger.

What Jesus does is to show that God's judgement

does not simply flow out of a moral code. It flows out of His immediate presence. Men have to live with God – God in His busyness with them in the world, as individuals and as groups.

The New Testament announces the result of this universal judgement of God in very simple terms: 'There is no just man, not one.' 'For in making all mankind prisoners to disobedience God's purpose was to show mercy to all mankind.' The working out of the one judgement is to serve as a preparation for and an incentive to man's acceptance of God's gift of mercy. The final purpose for all mankind is that it become and be a reconciled community. The germ of true living lies in learning to forgive and to be forgiven. It is the experience of God's judgement which brings men to the threshold of this encounter with God's mercy. This is why the proclamation of the gospel, the good news of God's forgiveness in Jesus Christ, has to be maintained in power and purity at the very heart of the historical movement. Judgement depends for its fruitfulness on the proclaimed mercy of God.

The New Testament confession is that salvation is by grace through faith. This means that grace must be accepted. He who is found guilty must accept that he is guilty and in need of forgiveness. He must agree to come to the light. He must be willing to accept that he is only a steward. He must ask for the insight and the ability to be brother-man. Men may not respond in this way and may refuse to accept God's offer of mercy. But, should they do this by pretending to themselves and before others that they actually stand in no need of mercy, then Jesus warned that they may, as sinners, arrive at the point of no return. There is no forgiveness, He said, for the sin against the Holy Spirit. To sin against Him was deliberately to argue onself into believing that evil was good and good was evil.

57

There is one other aspect of God's judgement which Jesus spoke about. 'Every tree which my Father has not planted', He said, 'will be rooted up.' Judgement is exercised not only over individuals and human societies, but also over the achievements of men. The salvation of secular history necessarily involves also the judgement of secular history. What, if tares and wheat grow together for a time! When harvest comes, the tares will be burnt and the wheat garnered. And then, the garnered wheat becomes seed for the next sowing. So history moves on through judgement and mercy, through condemnation and salvation, until He who is man's salvation becomes Himself immediately present reconciling the one God with the one humanity.

He existed before all things, and in union with Him all things have their proper place (Colossians 1:17).

One Destiny

God is one. He only is God who is the Father of Jesus Christ. It is not that there is one God behind and beyond a plurality of gods but that there is only one God, known in His particularity and yet also in His universality. His providence is for all equally, even though it is not the same kind of providence for all.

There is one history. The unity of this history is maintained and effected through an inner stream within it. The history of a particular people is determinative for history as a whole. The battle is for the few, victory is for the many. Only some are chosen for the mission even while all are included in the purpose. But this too needs to be said, that even though there are those who are distinguished from the rest as acknowledged partners in Christ's enterprise, yet it is He who decides who His partners will be and what instruments He will use.

58

His choice is not circumscribed either by religious allegiance or moral condition.

At the same time, within the breadth of His voice there is a visible missionary community who know that it is Him whom they serve and that it is by Him that they have been chosen. Within the ways in which He is building up a missionary community which will be a witness to His purpose and a token of that purpose's fulfilment. The task of this community is to proclaim the truth of God's action in Christ and to call men to repentance and faith in Him. However, this work of the gospel remains embedded in a pervasive process of judgement and redemption by which God makes His presence and will effective everywhere, to everyone, and always.

This way of confessing unity and difference, universality and particularity, at the same time, is what is peculiar to the Christian faith; and nowhere does this peculiar quality of the Christian faith become more evident than in the way in which it speaks of man's destiny.

In the last book of the Bible, three histories are brought to a common climax. There is the Book of Life in which are written the names of those who are the followers of the Lamb. As the seals of time are broken, they become increasingly revealed in their particularity and peculiarity. They are Christ's people, His bride. But the climax is not only the arrival of the Bridegroom to meet His bride. There is also a banquet. The symbolism of the banquet is intended to emphasize the fact that the climactic event of history includes a fulfilment which goes beyond the story of Christ's particular people.

The two symbols of bride and banquet are fused together when it is said that the New Jerusalem comes down from heaven. Men participate in the fulfilment of God's purposes on earth. But the final consummation is not a coping stone placed upon a building built from below. What God is actually doing through and in the midst of the confusions of history will stand revealed at the last as something which God only has done. And when that New Jerusalem comes, it will be a city into which the nations will bring their treasures, and in which they will find healing. The picture is the picture of a city with open gates on every side, gates which are not guarded and which are never closed, gates through which any can enter except those who will not come.

There is still one thing more to be said. For the Christian faith affirms not simply God's purpose to redeem the Church, mankind, human history, but also to redeem creation as a whole. 'The whole creation waits for its redemption.'

It is futile to protest that this whole picture presented of what it will be like when God has fulfilled His plan is so confused and confusing. Does not the challenge of the picture lie in holding together on one canvas different foci?

When God-with-man became man, He became man in Jesus Christ – a particular man who lived at a particular time in a particular place. This particularity persists in a particular community entrusted with a particular mission. That is one focus.

God is Creator and Father of all men. Jesus Christ is a man and the Redeemer and Judge of all men. The Holy Spirit is God at work in all men seeking to evoke repentance, obedience and faith. This is a second focus.

Each individual life has meaning within the life of the human community as a whole. Generations come and go but history goes on, and God's purpose is not only a purpose for the individual, not only a purpose for each generation, but a purpose for mankind's history. It is not simply men but history which is being redeemed. This is a third focus.

And finally, the total creation must come to its fulfilment. Nature has meaning not only in its relation to man and as serving his life, but also in its relation to God and as witnessing to His handiwork. The final glory is when all that God has made glorify Him. This is the fourth focus.

In Christian faith, life and obedience, attention is riveted, now on this focus and now on that. We may not for the sake of coherence seek to construct a premature synthesis which either blurs the distinctions or eliminates the contradictions.

Frankly, I stand amazed at the unfathomable complexity of God's wisdom and God's knowledge. How could man ever understand His reasons for action, or explain His methods of working? For of Him and through Him, and unto Him, are all things. To Him be the glory for ever, Amen (Romans 11:33–36).

I confess Jesus Christ:
God-with-man made flesh.
  His gift – the gift of faith in God;
  and, by Him, each man's faith
  made serviceable to fellow man.

All men meet in Him;
For, in Him, God and man are one.

He is God's fulfilment
  of every hope and need of man
and, because of Him,
on whose lordship everything depends,
  no loss is ever written off as final.

He comes as Servant:
  His service accepted setting men free to serve.
He comes as King:
  His equal rule investing life with wholeness.

Cognito and Incognito –
  and never the one without the other –
He comes constantly challenging discovery.

To discover Him
is to discover God and neighbour too;
  and in His continuing life
  find life with God and life with neighbour
  knit indissolubly into one.

Chapter Three

I Confess Jesus Christ

THE more one lives with the New Testament and its testimony to Jesus, the more one becomes aware of the dependence of the New Testament writers on what they knew to be the self-understanding of Jesus. And, when one turns to find out what Jesus did think of Himself and His mission, one finds that this is inextricably bound up with the way in which He understood scripture and saw there the form of obedience and faith to which it summoned Him.

A critical exposition of all the relevant texts, however, with a systematic study of the way in which the Lord's use of scripture underlay the formation of the christologies of the early church, would go beyond what is appropriate in a statement of faith. That which must be attempted rather, and which this chapter seeks to do, is to introduce the reader to a way of thought, without learning which, a good deal of the scriptural testimony to Jesus, both in the Old and New Testaments, must remain incomprehensible.

Through all the changing circumstances of life and in the midst of all its confusions, mystery and pain, it is Jesus who makes a Father-God credible. He keeps God safe for man. The faith, therefore, which affirms – 'I believe in God: God is One' – must of necessity disclose its rootedness in Him. However, the opposite necessity exists also: to reverse, as it were, the direction of sight and look at Jesus Christ from one's point of arrival in God. From Jesus was launched and by Him was powered the journey to God; but once arrived and faith in God established, the return journey has to be made. Jesus needs to be confessed directly as part of one's testament of faith.

St Paul, writing to his adopted son Timothy, commends him for confessing his faith nobly and publicly before many witnesses. 'I charge you,' he says, 'in the presence of God and of Christ Jesus, who before Pilate nobly witnessed to His faith, never to blot your copybook, but to obey your orders until the Lord Jesus Christ appears.' The confession made by Jesus is the original which Timothy must copy. Both copy and original will be vindicated when Jesus himself appears.

Or, to put the matter the other way round, by one particular person at one particular place – Jesus Christ before Pontius Pilate – man's faith in God was confessed in its full import. Here was made clear that no other 'rule' was ultimate, and that God alone was God, and that on this faith the whole of life could be staked. Now, the Christian stands where Jesus stood, confessing Him; and so appropriating His confession as the Christian's own. The result is the living of the confessing life, in which one is delivered from the ambiguities and generalities of the religious life, and committed to the specific and concrete demands of personal discipleship. He who confessess Christ becomes the kind of person whose own life is inexplicable apart from Christ.

In New Testament teaching, the act of confession and the attitude of confessing are set out in a variety of ways. It may be enough here to look at the instances in which the word itself is used. As will become evident, the usage always is such as to point beyond Jesus to the Father; and to point to Jesus as the 'only' of the Father. The relationship between Father and Son is the heart of any true confession of Jesus.

'Every one who confesses me before men, I also will confess before my Father who is heaven.' This saying of Jesus is related to His teaching that men should live unafraid because God is their Father, a Father who cares for every sparrow. 'You will acknowledge the Father', says Jesus, 'by acknowledging me. If you confess me, that is if you show to the world that you belong to me, then you will find that I shall show you that you belong to the Father.' Only Jesus can make the varied experiences of life, ways to the Father, for only He comes from the Father along the road of these experiences.

'And every tongue confess, Jesus Christ is Lord, to the glory of God the Father.' Here St Paul makes the Christian confession the consequence of an event. 'Jesus Christ made himself nothing, assumed the nature of a slave, bore the human likeness, in obedience accepted death. Therefore God raised him to the heights.' The moment of confession is when this Incarnation and Exaltation become the standing ground of faith. Jesus is Lord whether one likes it or not, knows it or not, acknowledges it or not. Because He is Lord, one believes and confesses.

'Whoever confesses that Jesus is the Son of God, God abides in him and he in God.' In the passage in which this verse occurs, St John is controverting those who make the name of Jesus Christ a platform for their own opinions. He insists that truly to confess Jesus is to confess Him in His particularity – 'Jesus Christ has come in the flesh.' To abide in God was to find God in this man, and to have received His Spirit was to know that it was God himself who wrought the response of faith. When this is so, says St John, how can anyone

attempt to make the Lord he confesses a front for his own speculations or even piety!

'Since then we have a great high priest, Jesus the Son of God, let us hold fast our confession.' The writer of the letter to the Hebrews, puts his emphasis on what happens to the person who confesses. He is led along the way that Jesus walked: for God, 'in bringing many sons to glory, made the pioneer of their salvation perfect through suffering'. Or, to put it more directly, the confessing life leads one into the experience of Jesus himself, who learned obedience through what He suffered, who was tempted yet without sinning, whose prayers and petitions were heard which with loud cries and tears He offered up.

'I know who you are. You are the Christ of the living God.' This confession of St Peter at Caesarea Philippi is basic: and the responses of Jesus to it:

* Simon, by this confession and because of it, you yourself will be changed: you will become Peter.
* That you made this confession about me shows that you know my Father too: only He could have revealed me to you.
* This confession and those who confess it will always be the bedrock of the Church: a confessing Church cannot be destroyed.
* But more than that, such a Church will itself attack the strongholds of evil, and the gates of hell cannot withstand it.
* You will come to see that to confess in this way implies suffering and rejection both for the Christ you confess, and for yourself who confess Him.
* The devil will constantly suggest to you that this suffering can be avoided: remember that I said, it cannot be.

He who confesses the Son, has the Father also (I John 2:23)

Carpenter - Confessor

Who is He – this Jesus whom I confess?

Jesus was a carpenter. That was His trade and occupation. He helped His father Joseph in his carpentry shop; and later when His father died, He conducted the business himself. In Nazareth, the village in which He grew up, He was well known. When He returned there as a preacher and teacher, they said to one another 'Is this not *the* carpenter?' Perhaps His was the best known carpenter's shop in the village. Is it fancy to think that over that carpenter's shop hung a board which said, 'My yoke is easy'. He made good and smooth yokes not only because he was a good carpenter, but also because He cared about the oxen for whom the yokes were meant.

This carpenter, at the age of thirty, became a wanderer, without fixed abode. He walked out, as it were, on to the road and met life as it came. He went into a synagogue on the sabbath and preached. He walked through the corn-fields and found in the situation that developed an opportunity to expound the scriptures. He halted a funeral procession and raised the dead to life. He went to a wedding and provided wine for the feast. A leper came to Him and He touched him. A blind man cried for help and He healed him. The teachers of the law found Him wandering around the temple courts and engaged Him in controversy. It was a most unsystematic life: just a life lived with men and among men in the midst of life's pre-occupations.

But that precisely was what Jesus was: a man among men. He was not a teacher or preacher as such. He was identified wherever he went simply by the surprise of His humanity. He said and did unexpected things. His presence in any situation gave to it a new dimension.

He lifted life to new possibilities. He claimed that this was so, because in Him God's rule had come within the reach of men. He said that His own mission was so to live and work and die as to enable men to find in Him the possibility of coping with the consequences of this breaking in of the rule of God.

No wonder that Jesus does not fit into any of the normal categories of preacher, teacher, prophet, saint, philosopher, revolutionary. Indeed, has not every attempt made since even to say that this is what He taught on any particular subject proved ephemeral? Nor have men succeeded in deducing from His teachings what can be called general principles. The fact is that there is only one way of finding out what in any situation His teaching is, and that is to know Him in the actuality of the life He lived and then to accompany with Him in the life He is living now. There is no way of divorcing what Jesus teaches from His living presence, nor is there any way of knowing Him as He is except by knowing Him as He was. In the gospels, the story practically begins in the middle. A man appears among His fellow-men at the river Jordan and takes His place as one of them within a movement of religious revival. As the story develops, its characteristic is the ways in which this man became part and parcel of life as it was actually being lived all around Him. The record is of the things He said and did as He participated in the actual business of living. But, as the gospels tell the story, little by little, because of what He said and did, men began to ask the question as to who He was. This question increasingly dominates the narrative until the climax is reached when He is arrested and put on trial.

When one reads the story of the trial of Jesus, one is struck by the fact that He was not accused of any wrong He had done. Even to the blunt and direct question of Pilate: 'What wrong has He done?' there was no answer. What the trial reveals is that Jesus was crucified because of who He said He was. In the trial before the Sanhedrin, the issue was as to what He meant by saying that He would replace the temple with His body. In the trial before the High Priest, there was the direct question and answer: 'Are you the Christ?' – 'I am'. In the trial before Pilate, the accusation was that Jesus claimed to be King.

What men found irksome and increasingly impossible to tolerate was the way in which He not only made certain claims for Himself, but also acted on the basis of these claims. He sought to set aside the structure of religion as He found it among His contemporaries – I am the temple. He made demands over men's lives which only God had a right to make – I am the Christ. He lived as a free citizen of God's Kingdom and as representative of the King. And yet withal, He lived – a man among men – and so completely at men's mercy that they not only could reject Him but also eliminate Him. Jesus presented men with the opportunity of rejecting God, and they took it. There is no other way of reading the gospel story.

The carpenter and the confessor were integrally one: hence the issue. On the one hand was the carpenter with His inexplicable claims; while on the other hand, if His claims were true, was the man in the puzzling ordinariness of His life. Those who did not believe in Him had to contend with His claims, whereas those who did believe in Him had to contend with His life. Unbeliever and believer alike had a mystery to contend with. He attended the synagogue every sabbath day, He went to the temple of Jerusalem for its feasts, He paid the temple tax. What did He mean by saying: 'Destroy this temple.' He prayed regularly and incessantly, He spoke of being tempted, His constant reference was to God as Father, His piety was so thoroughly human. How was He the Christ? He had power and authority which He hardly used. He performed no wonders that others before Him had not performed, He made no protest however harsh His humiliation. What kind of a King was He?

Men sensed a contradiction in Jesus which would not leave them alone. They were unable just to treat him as a man and let it go at that. What, then, were they to do?

Blessed is he who takes no offence at me (Luke: 7:23).

Son of Man - Son of God

Matthew, Mark and Luke tell the story of Jesus as it developed. The question of 'who He is' is kept in the background, except that from the very beginning can be heard the murmur of the crowd as they discuss among themselves who Jesus was. Who was this teacher so unlike the scribes? Who was this wonder-worker so unlike the prophets? Who was this authority so unlike the priests? John, however, tells the story from the very beginning in the light of Jesus' identity. Every episode is illuminated by who Jesus is. John's concern is to communicate the meaning of what happened; while the attempt of the synoptists is to tell the story as it happened, and as it made it's impact on those who saw and heard.

Here lies the key to the use of the term 'Son of Man' as it is found in the synoptic gospels, where Jesus is reported as constantly referring to himself in this way. In John's gospel, the consistent designation of Jesus is as the Son – the Son of the Father – so that whenever the term 'Son of Man' is used, it is already iridescent with fuller meaning. In the synoptists however, it is a term which invites discovery. A story is being told, but the person, about whom the story is, is more than meets the eye: and that 'more' is communicated by the many undertones and implications of the title 'Son of Man' by which He is designated. Therefore, it is to the use of this term in scripture primarily, and in current literature at the time of Jesus, that attention must be paid to gain an understanding of what it means and what it was intended to signify.

What is man that you are mindful of him.
and the son of man that you care for him   (Ps. 8:4)

The Son of man is just a man. Why did Jesus have to keep reminding the people that He was one of them. There is an incident recorded in the Acts of the Apostles concerning Paul and Barnabas at Listra in which, because the people thought they were gods, they had to establish their identity as men. Jesus had to do this throughout His life.

He raised questions in people's minds. Could He be the Christ? How could He claim to forgive sins? By what authority did He set aside the laws of the Sabbath? Did not wind and wave obey Him! He responded to this situation by saying, 'I am man'; and by living a transparently human life among them.

Lest Your hand be upon the man of Your right hand,
the son of man whom You have made strong for
Yourself (Ps. 80:17).

The son of man is the man for others. God will work for others through Him. Jesus made this claim in no uncertain terms. He has come to do for men what they could not do for themselves. 'Unless I wash you, you have no part with me. I am come that you may have life and have it in full measure. I am the light of the world: if you walk in my light, you will not stumble. I am the door of the sheepfold: through me you come into safety, through me you go out to pasture. I am the good shepherd: I lay down my life for the sheep.'

71

To be the son of man was to be man to men – the possibility and potency of their true humanity.

Son of man, stand upon your feet, and I will speak with you.

I send you ... and you shall speak my words (Ezek. 2:1–7).

The son of man is man under God's address. He is to men God's word to them. There is nothing more striking in the gospel narrative than the stories which are given of the conversations of Jesus with people. In every case, the essential point of each story is not a piece of teaching couched in general terms but a specific command or comment. 'Let the dead bury the dead. Go and bring your husband. Sell what you have and give it to the poor. Who made me a judge between you and your brother. Let him without sin cast the first stone. Leave your nets and follow me.'

General truth explodes in concrete demand. The authority of God over a person's life is pressed home. The son of man is the locale of God's word, work and visitation.

As Moses lifted up the serpent in the wilderness, so must the son of man be lifted up (John. 3:1).

The son of man is representative man. The meanings of the phrase 'son of man' in the Old Testament show what echo the use of this phrase by Jesus would have caused in the hearts and minds of His hearers. But Jesus meant even more than all this. He thought of himself as that man in whom God's action of deliverance was performed for all men.

He recalled two incidents in the Exodus story to make the point. The son of man would be as the brazen serpent: representative of God's judgement on sin and man's deliverance from it. He would also be as the manna, provided by God, on whose representative life

men would be nourished and sustained in their pilgrimage.

> *With clouds of heaven, there came one like a son of*
> *man,*
> *and to him was given dominion and glory and king-*
> *dom*   (Dan. 3 : 13–14)

The son of man is he who is to come. It was the
designation given to the One who, at the end, would
bring all things to their consummation; who would
reap the harvest of history.

It is of this son of man that Stephen spoke. 'I can
see,' he said, 'the son of man standing at God's right
hand.' Only a few minutes earlier, he had been witnessing to Jesus. Now as he dies, he says to those who kill
him: 'It is with this Jesus that the final word lies, it is
to Him that I go.' Here, in personal terms, is the confession of Jesus as life's destination. Living and dying,
in Jesus God is found. That is the Christian confession.

The Lord became flesh – very man. But those who
saw Him, saw a glory which belonged to God alone.
Jesus was man as man ought to be. Hence the exclamation of the Roman Centurion who saw Him die:

> *Truly this man was the Son of God* (Mark 15 : 39).

Servant – Lord

Three issues gather round the confession of Jesus:
Who was He? How was He to be accepted? What
were the consequences of thus accepting Him?

His was an ordinary human life. He had to be discerned through it. He hungered and slept, He went to
funerals and weddings. He played with children in the
market-place and dined with friends in their homes.
He showed anger and compassion, He wept and
laughed. But He came, as He said, to announce God's

73

kingdom, and to be among men the proof that it had come.

The coming of God's kingdom, however, was not an event alongside other events. It was an event within all other events. Hence the form of His testimony to God's kingdom through normal participation in ordinary life. It was thus that, in Him, men met the kingdom in purpose and in power; and saw what its consequences were in the simple business of living. But precisely here was the difficulty of answering the question which He raised as to how men were to accept Him: for having raised the question, He made the answer dependent on an understanding of the ways, in which He Himself understood and declared His role in relation to the kingdom – ways of thought completely wedged within the structure of Jewish faith and practice.

The controlling testimony to the nature of God as one finds it in the Old Testament is to the faithfulness of His love. He is faithful to His creation and to every part of it. 'He is good to the earth, watering her furrows. The valleys stand thick with corn, they laugh and sing. The lions too seek their meat from God. He even feeds the ravens, unclean birds though they are. Because of Him, the great whales out in the ocean play for joy.' This faithfulness of God is also to every nation and people, every race and kindred. All the lands are part of His care. He blesses and punishes, He admonishes and chastises, He suffers with and for and by: but he never gives up. He remains faithful, always Immanuel.

Such a faithfulness needs a demonstration that will be convincing; a disclosure with someone to disclose it to. That is the basis of the peculiar history of Abraham and his descendants. They were to be the means of making God's faithfulness known in all the world and to every people. They would be the explicit, though not the exclusive instrument of God's working. To use a double figure, God's covenant with a particular people sets up within the human story a place of illumination which lights up that story as a whole; there flows within the broad river of human history an inner compulsive current.

According to the biblical record, when the climactic moment of disclosure arrived, Israel was in exile in Babylon, with its city and temple in ruins in Jerusalem. Israel had proved faithless to God's purpose. But since God was faithful, He would neither let Israel go nor compromise His demands. He decreed to bring Israel back to obedience through suffering, even though it had to be suffering unto death. But why punish Israel, when the nations for whose sake Israel was called were worse than Israel itself? The reason was in the result. For when, by suffering, Israel would be fitted for its vocation and fulfilled it, then the nations would acknowledge Israel as having paid the price of their peace. Indeed, having suffered at the hands of the nations, Israel would in return become their source of blessing.

This relation of Israel to the nations was equally true within Israel: for since suffering had come on all Israel, faithless and faithful alike, the suffering of the faithful would lift the suffering borne into a larger-fulfilment. The faithful suffered because they belonged with the rest and had no desire except so to belong. Israel was servant to the nations, the faithful in Israel were servant to the faithless among them. In each case the badge of the servant was that he was at the mercy of those whom he served.

Jesus asked that He be accepted in this role of servant; as the One in whom and by whom, through suffering unto obedience, God's purpose to bless and redeem would be fulfilled. He would be Israel, through whom the nations would be blessed. He would also be the true Israel, through whom Israel as a whole would come to its destiny. Israel's expectation of the Messiah was as the One who would vindicate God within the processes of history. Jesus saw that the Messiah had to be, at the same time, the person in whom, as a person, God's faithfulness was vindicated. In one life Christ-hood and Servant-hood must meet.

Here was the insight which the disciples and contemporaries of Jesus found so confusing. They could not understand the necessity on which He insisted when He said that the Christ must suffer. Why 'must'? Because His obedience was to be what, in Him, those who confess Him would become.

Jesus insisted that He was Lord always and only in the sense that He had the right to claim men as His own. They belonged to Him and He was the true master of their lives. But if they were at His disposal, it was because He was at their service. He would make them what he called them to be. He would engage them in His mission, but they would work with Him and in His company. He would call them to suffering, but only in fellowship with His own. He would give them tasks beyond their powers, and they would know the power of His resurrection at work in their lives. His lordship would know Him as Lord through that which His service in them and for them would accomplish.

'The Christ must suffer' because He is the Christ, and because through the ages He must exercise that Christhood.

The Son of Man did not come to be served but to serve, and to surrender his life as a ransom for many (Mark 10:45).

Priest – King

Is not Jesus every man's contemporary? Why not then seek to understand Him as He is? Why seek to solve the puzzles of His relation to His scriptures? Why not just read the story of His life as it is given in the gospels, and reflect on it directly?

The simple fact is that the gospels do not give what can be called the story of His life. What they give is testimony – the words and works of Jesus; and those events in His life to which attention is drawn because they are the facts on which the testimony is based. As the fourth gospel has it, 'Those here written have been recorded in order that you may hold the faith that Jesus is the Christ, the Son of God, and that through this faith you may possess eternal life by His name'. And their testimony, the gospel writers rest unhesitatingly on the testimony of the scriptures to Jesus Christ concerning whom, according to Jesus Himself, these scriptures speak. 'You search the scriptures', He had said, 'because you think that in them you have eternal life; and it is they that bear witness to me.' As it is recorded in the Emmaus story: 'He began with Moses and all the prophets, and explained to them the passages which referred to himself in every part of the scriptures.'

The scriptures give the story of God's covenant with man, both in its universality – with all men – and in its particularity – with Israel – the covenant to be Immanuel. This covenant became fleshly truth in Jesus Christ and remains, in Jesus Christ, man's continuing situation. Jesus Christ sets up the magnetic field within which the place and position of the various parts of scripture, like iron filings, are determined. Of course, the problem is that the magnet which is Jesus Christ is

77

not in any one's hands to wield. No man's biblical exposition is final. Indeed, while the Bible is infallible in its witness to Him, that infallible witness is in no one's keeping.

To disregard the scriptures, therefore, would be to disregard the testimony on which alone a confession of Jesus can be based. As St. Paul puts it: 'These are the facts imparted to me: that Christ died for our sins, in accordance with the scriptures; that he was buried; that he was raised to life on the third day, according to the scriptures; and that he appeared . . .'

Naturally, there is illumination at many levels. First of all, there are the terms, of which 'Son of Man' is just one example, which come to their concreteness in Jesus of Nazareth. Secondly, there are the concepts, as that of 'Servant', which grow out of Israel's national and religious history which find their fulfilment in who Jesus was and how He lived and died. And thirdly, there is the very structure of the scriptures which is realized in Jesus and, therefore, points to Him as the substance of which it is the shadow. Law and law-giver, temple and priest, word and prophet, kingdom and king: this is basic structure. What happens in Jesus is that the law is made dependent on grace, the temple is replaced by His broken body, the Word becomes flesh, and the kingdom is inaugurated as the kingdom of the Father. Lawgiver, priest, prophet and king were mediators, each in his own way, of God's covenant with His people. In Jesus mediacy gives way to immediacy, and the covenant is seen in its fullness as compassing all men and not just Israel.

God's faithfulness and man's obedience – these are the two sides of the covenant between God and man. Scripture asserted that the Messiah would be the final expression of God's faithfulness; and that, on man's side, obedience would be finally wrought by him who was the suffering servant. In Jesus, God's faithfulness and man's obedience came together in one life. Hence the immediacy which lies in Him. He is God to men – the remedy for the defilement of sin; and man to God – pleading men's cause before the Father. 'We have one to plead our cause with the Father, I mean Jesus Christ – and He is good. He himself is the sacrifice, by which the defilement of our sins is removed.'

The writer of the Epistle to the Hebrews uses the figure of Melchizedek to give point and precision to this aspect of the meaning of Jesus. Melchizedek was a secular figure. He was the King of Salem. He was outside the call of Abraham. But, as the story in Genesis has it, Abraham brought the spoils of his victory and laid them before Melchizedek. He acknowledged Melchizedek as priest of the most high God. Here was a priesthood outside the Aaronic priesthood, a priesthood welded to the secular and not to the sacred, a priesthood which belonged to no succession. Jesus is Priest and King according to the order of Melchizedek, says the writer to the Hebrews. He cannot be contained in any sacred history, His credentials lie in no geneology. Offering brought to Him is for the service of the world of which He is King: and because He is Priest as well, God is found and known in Him not only in the sacred relationships of the covenant but also in the ordinary ways of secular life.

'You are a royal priesthood,' says St Peter, writing to his fellow Christians. He seeks to make them understand what that calling means. It means to be that community in the world within which God's rule and presence are immediately experienced. St Peter is not thinking of the priesthood of the temple; he is thinking of Jesus' own priesthood directly exercised in the world of which He is also King.

Truly to confess Jesus, therefore, means to accept

79

Him in this His priesthood and kingship, and so be delivered from every bondage and boundary which the 'sacred' will constantly seek to impose upon one's life. Not that the sacred is left behind or denied, but that it is offered to Him for whom the secular and the sacred are one. He who is according to the scriptures lifts them to another plane of fulfilment.

The law has but a shadow of the good things to come instead of the true form of these realities (Hebrews 10:1).

Promise – Fulfilment

The truth of Jesus Christ as the second meaning of scripture has one further dimension to it. He fulfils its promise.

'Behold, the days are coming, says the Lord, when I will make a new covenant with the house of Israel and the house of Judah, not like the covenant which I made with their fathers which they broke ... I will put my law within them, and I will write it upon their hearts; and I will be their God, and they shall be my people. And no longer shall each man teach his neighbour saying, "Know the Lord", for they shall all know me. I will forgive their iniquity, and I will remember their sin no more.'

The covenant through the law would be transcended: not that this covenant was wrong or ineffective in the first place, but that the time would come when its intention could be fulfilled. The long experience of the community under the law would become the interior possession of each individual within the community. Also the grace of a changed heart which was the experience of the faithful through succeeding generations would become the established basis of relationship between God and the community as a whole.

80

Israel was God's vineyard. He had planted and tended it: but it had yielded only wild grapes. Jesus said, 'I am the true vine. The branch that abides in me will bear good fruit.' But how was this abiding to be accomplished? He said that it would be accomplished by what He would do through His death. His words were, 'The New Covenant shall be sealed by my blood.'

The blood of the sacrifice represented the offered life of the person who made the sacrifice. Jesus was man offering His life to God in perfect and humble obedience. Through Him men have direct access to God, His obedience pulsing through them producing in them the fruits of obedience also. The tables of the law which were the means of the Old Covenant taught the nature of the obedience which God demanded. The offered life of Christ which is the means of the New Covenant effects that obedience. Men participate in His continuing life and are changed into His likeness.

The death of Jesus is compared by St Paul to the slaying of the passover lamb. The fourth evangelist makes clear that it was on passover eve that Jesus died, himself slain when the passover lambs would be slain for the passover feast. 'Eat your passover with unleavened bread,' St Paul says, 'having purged out the leaven of corruption. For indeed our passover has begun, the sacrifice is offered – Christ himself.' The figure of feeding on Jesus, which St Paul uses, is of course derived from Jesus himself. He had said, 'As I live because of the Father, so he who eats me will live because of me.' 'The bread is my body broken for you.'

The symbolism is clear. His death marks the dividing line between the old bondage and the new freedom. By Him is the possibility of new life. He becomes the available One in whom forgiveness for the past and renewal for the future are established. The assurance of forgiveness is in the fact that His life is offered to and for sinners while they are yet sinners.

The cry of Jesus, 'My God! My God! why have you forsaken me', is the sinner's cry. He stood where sinners stand, experiencing the judgment of God on sin and the wrath of God on the sinner. But precisely here is the turning of the sinner to God: for it is to God that the cry of dereliction is addressed. When the sinner stands where Jesus stood, he finds himself carried beyond the experience of judgement and wrath into the experience of being forgiven. He is turned towards God. Jesus makes possible the faith which discovers God's love and clings to Him at the very moment of condemnation.

In St John's gospel, the offered life of Jesus by which men are nourished and the outpoured life of Jesus in which men are cleansed are brought together in a significant symbolism. When the soldier standing by the cross pierced the side of Jesus with a spear, St John says that he himself saw that water and blood gushed out. The note of personal testimony is emphatic. What St John intends to convey seems to be that just as every communion cup is filled with the blood that flowed from Jesus' side, so is every baptismal font filled from the water that flowed from that side also. The New Covenant is the covenant of a new birth and a new beginning made firm in a forgiveness which is always at work.

At the heart of Jeremiah's prophecy is the promise, 'I will be their God and they shall be my people'. Here is renewed God's promise to Abraham. What God wants is to create a people who will demonstrate what it means to belong to Him and to belong to Him alone. The thrust of the promise is not that He belongs to them in any exclusive way but that they belong to Him exclusively. Their quality as His possession will be seen in their knowledge of Him. 'No longer shall each man teach his neighbour saying, "Know the Lord", for they shall all know me.'

The Holy Spirit is the source of this inward assurance. In St John's epistle, the witnesses to the person and work of Jesus are listed as 'the water, the blood and the Spirit'. According to St John's gospel, Jesus came to baptize with the Holy Spirit: and the gospel story reaches its climax when after His resurrection, He breathed on His disciples and said, 'Receive the Holy Spirit'. The yoke of the law with its burdensomeness could now be set aside. Instead, there could be taken the yoke of the Son, a yoke which was good to bear, whose load was light. And with the law would go also the whole system of sacrifices. For, as Jesus said, His body was the new temple: a temple in which the sacrifice offered by the disciple would be his own life.

Abide in me ... for apart from me you can do nothing (John 15:4–5).

Cognito – Incognito

Since faith is what God looks for. His approach to men has to be consonant with that expectation. There can be no overwhelming miracle which puts reason to flight nor an appeal so overpowering that the will consents because it has been flushed out by emotion. Hence the truth about Jesus that 'he really and truly became a servant, and was made for a time exactly like men. In a human form that all could see, he accepted such a depth of humiliation that he was prepared to die, and to die on a cross.'

This incognito of Christ is a continuing reality. The risen and ascended Lord remains incognito even now.

The way the resurrection stories are reported underline this truth. The risen Lord made himself known to the eyes of faith alone. As before, He would not take the citadel of the human heart by storm.

In the parable of the last judgement in which the sheep and the goats are separated, the crux of the parable lies in the presence of the Christ incognito. Those who had accepted Him did not know that it was Him they had accepted, while those who had rejected Him had not recognized Him either. It is Jesus who decides the form and the event in which He will present himself for acceptance: and how often He does it without disclosing His name! The parable makes the further point too, that those who did His will did not know whose will they were doing. Can it be that in telling this story as a parable concerning the judgement of the nations, Jesus is making the point that there will be those working for wholeness in human relationships who do not know that it is Christ's will for man which they are thereby fulfilling? The Christ incognito is acknowledged by deed, but it is the Christ that is acknowledged. 'He who has my commandments and keeps them, he it is who loves me; and I will love him and manifest myself to him.'

St Paul, in his speech to the men of Athens, says to them: 'I can identify for you your Unknown God.' He is not saying that he can tell them the true name and nature of the gods they worship. These they already knew: Jupiter and Juno, Venus and Neptune, Mercury and Mars. But their religious experience had overflowed their religious system, and it was this over-spill which they had identified by erecting an altar to the Unknown God. St Paul says to them, I want to speak to you about this Unknown God who has caused this

84

over-spill in your lives. It is He who is God. In Him you live and move and have your being. His presence and power in you and among you is what has caused you to set up an altar to Him even though you do not know His name. Actually, you can know who He is by the fact that it is to Him that you are ultimately accountable: He himself having appointed the person who will act as judge at the last, a judgement beyond death, and therefore the appointed judge declared to be so by being raised from the dead already.

But the Christ incognito is not only a fact for those who do not as yet acknowledge Him Lord, He is also so for those who do. Among those who did not recognize their encounter with Jesus when He came to them in a marginal person in society – the poor, the imprisoned, the stranger – were persons who had already accepted Him as Lord. For the disciples of Jesus, the problem always will remain of how to identify those situations and challenges in which He waits for them, since it is incognito that He waits. In that other parable in which Jesus speaks of those who had exercised their discipleship in the accepted ways – they had preached, healed, and served in His name – Jesus makes himself say, 'I never knew you'. They are not rejected because, as it were, a debit account is set over against their credit account. They are rejected because they never were in truth His disciples. The success which attended their ministry was simply due to the presence of the Christ in others.

There is a further thought about the Christ incognito in relation to His disciples which is important, and that is with respect to the explicit promise of His presence which He has made. 'Where two or three are gathered in my name, there am I in the midst of them.' And yet how difficult it is to discern His presence in the little prayer meetings, parish councils and church assemblies! How human these are; how tragically involved in petty squabbles, group selfishness, and rivalries about place and position! And yet His presence is there, the presence which has been promised, and to be discerned in His judgements which are at work, in His rule and over-rule which keeps the goals of His purpose alive, and in His mercy and patience which keep providing time for obedience.

Besides, what of His presence in the central act of the Church's worship, in word and sacrament? Here too His presence is incognito, a presence which can neither be manipulated nor made secure. The preached word is human speech seeking to bear testimony to that Word made flesh. However, on the working of the Holy Spirit will depend whether His word is actually heard. 'The wind blows as it lists.' Also, how many unnecessary theological controversies have been the result of the anxiety to celebrate what came to be called 'a valid sacrament'! As if there was some kind of ascertainable connection between the Church's ordering of the sacrament of Holy Communion and the Lord's decision to give Himself to His people! The Christ is present to faith alone, and faith alone apprehends and responds.

Finally, there is His presence to be discerned in the movements of human history: the history of thought and culture of religion and ethics, of science and technology, of lands and peoples – movements in which He is present as the Lord who creates and condemns, using as the instruments of His purpose whomever He wills, and drawing men to faithful response to His beckoning whatever be the way in which that beckoning is experienced or explained. So He leads those who follow, each to his own Calvary, and from there to sharing with Him in the victory of Easter.

The steward tasted the water now turned into wine, not knowing its source; though the servants who had drawn the water knew (John 2:9).

CHAPTER FOUR

Jesus is Lord

I BELIEVE in God. God is one. I confess Jesus Christ
Jesus is Lord.

No sooner does one believe in God, the Father, than
one goes on to affirm something about His work and
His nature. God is one. No sooner does one confess
Jesus Christ than one goes to find that He is Lord of
all life. Often we state the case wrongly when we say
that Christ belongs to all men. The question rather is
whether we belong to Christ. If He is master and Lord,
then we can have no other in our lives. All that we know
is that His yoke is easy and His burden is light.

Belief in God is reflected in the oneness of the universe. It is all in one piece with one underlying plan or
motif. The confession of the Lordship of Christ is reflected in the obedience of the Church. It goes further
than that, for even those who do not know yet are still
being brought into the vortex of a common history, of
a common life, as He builds up the human family under
one head.

The earlier confession of the Christian community was:
'Jesus is Lord.' It was the confession under which they
were baptised and the confession with which they died.
It was the burden of the hymns they sang when they
were thrown to the lions in the Roman amphitheatre.

It was the faith by which they lived in the catacombs.

Jesus saw Himself in His scriptures. The scriptures decided for Him the message He proclaimed, the mission He undertook, the obedience He rendered. For the disciples, however, the primary experience was of Jesus himself, and the primary issue their own personal relation to Him. The gospels show how in their companionship with Him the disciples finally adopted the title 'Lord' as the most appropriate to express what He was to them. 'You call me Master and Lord, and rightly so, for that is what I am.'

Jesus had rightful authority over their lives: He was not 'Lord' because they accepted Him as such, but because that was what he really was. 'To this end Christ died and lived again, that He might be Lord both of the dead and of the living.' The confession of Jesus as Lord is misstated where the implication is that He is Lord only of those who accept Him as such. The testimony of apostolic teaching is that He has been declared 'Lord' by and through His resurrection and ascension: so that when men accepted Him as Lord they are simply coming to terms with reality. 'You will be saved when you confess with your lips that Jesus is Lord and believe in your heart that God raised Him from the dead.' There is no other safe foundation for one's life.

The title 'Lord' had a double thrust – a scriptural and a secular one. The proper name for God in the scriptures was Yahweh. In the Greek, this name was translated as Lord. The concept of Yahweh was that of God in living action. He was the God of Abraham, of Moses, of David, of the prophets. He was the God of Israel's history, and for the Israelite, therefore, the Lord of all history. When Peter said, 'Thou art the Christ, the son of the living God', it was this confession that he was making. 'We know that when the Christ comes, that will be God's decisive action in history. You are that event.'

But Jesus was more than a particular event. By His continuing association with Him, all men being as His contemporaries with the impact of His Lordship upon their lives. He continues, God is living action: His action and activity are for the salvation and consummation of all things.

The secular thrust of the term 'Lord' came from the nature of the world at that time. It was a world in which men in differing relationships had the ultimate power of life and death over their fellows; masters over slaves, husbands over their mistresses, fathers over their children, Caesar over his subjects. The term for this ultimate authority was 'Lord'. In this kind of world, the early followers of Jesus proclaimed that there was only one Lord – Jesus, and that, in the last analysis, it was to Him alone that everyone belonged and was accountable.

When the Roman emperors began to take to themselves divine titles, and Caesar worship became an imperial institution, 'Jesus is Lord' became the battle cry of the Christians. 'Jesus has been enthroned' was what they said. God not only raised Him up from the dead, but also exalted Him at His right hand. He has been appointed ruler over this age: a rule He exercises now and will consummate hereafter.

An immediate presence, the ultimate authority – a risen and ascended Lord – that was the axis of the apostolic proclamation. No wonder, at Thessalonica, the disciples of Christ were accused of 'turning the world upside down', of 'acting against the decrees of Caesar by saying that there is another King, Jesus'.

The Christian story makes little sense when Christianity is looked upon merely as a religion. There are many religions and each teaches a particular way of understanding reality. They set down practices of worship, meditation and ritual to effect moral cleansing and spiritual growth. They inculcate the rightfulness of a certain kind of life and challenge men to seek certain goals for human society. Christianity shares these characteristics, but its essential feature is not that it seeks to be a religion, but rather that it seeks to convey to all men the news that there is a vast enterprise on, an enterprise in which they are all involved, irrespective of their own decisions concerning it. They share in the enterprise, they can rebel against it, but they cannot be out of it. To confess Jesus as Lord is to acknowledge that this news is true, to undertake the responsibility of making it known, and to share in the enterprise knowingly, obediently and joyfully.

In the Acts of the Apostles, there are two speeches of St Peter, which come at the very beginning of the record, which between them strike out the major themes of the Christian story. The story and what it means are the ground from which the Christian confession springs and on which it rests. What happened?

Jesus of Nazareth was a man attested by God by miracles and deeds which were amazing demonstrations of divine power in action. God was acting through him, and you, Men of Israel, saw it. This man was handed over to you, and you handed him over to Pilate, repudiating Him. When Pilate's judgement was that he should be released, you killed the man who blazed the way that leads to life by having him crucified by heathen men who had no knowledge of the Law of God. But God brought him back to life again, for it was impossible that he should remain under death's control. That God resurrected this Jesus is a fact of which we have personal knowledge, which we can personally guarantee. You acted in ignorance, but this was God's way of fulfilling everything which he foretold through the

91

prophets that the Messiah should suffer. Now he has been exalted to the right hand of God. Heaven must receive him until the time of the restoration of all things. So, then, repent and turn to God, if you want the record of your sins to be blotted out, if you want to enjoy times of refreshment sent by the Lord, and if you want him to send the Messiah, whom he has already appointed – Jesus.

Conceived by the Holy Ghost, Born of the Virgin Mary

The Christian community has a proclamation to make. There is the news to be announced which concerns all men and which, therefore, all men must hear. Something has happened of decisive importance. God has acted in a new way. He had always been active within His creation; now He has acted in such a way as to insert within it a new beginning. When creation came into being, it was the work of the Holy Spirit. The Spirit of God brooded over chaos, and chaos responded to God's command. Once again, conceived by the Holy Spirit, a new creation has taken place: this man – Jesus. In the speech of St Peter on the day of Pentecost, it is on this fact that the first emphasis falls. 'God did this thing.'

The phrase, 'conceived by the Holy Ghost', in the Apostles Creed, is theology and not biology. It states the link between Jesus Christ and everything that went before Him and everything that will come after Him. Cosmos was wrested from chaos. But the turbulence of chaos remained, an active force constantly to be contended. There was always a challenge against which the Holy Spirit had to maintain His creation. It was like a contest between light and darkness: the light shining and the darkness failing to extinguish it. The mid-point in the history of this contest between light and darkness is Jesus. He is the light itself. The proclamation to all men now is that the light has come.

In the story of Jesus which follows, the Holy Spirit is mentioned again in connection with His temptations in the wilderness. The river which, in the secrecy of the hills, had its source in the springs of the spirit, is now by that same spirit being guided into the flat-land where people dwell. Where this decisive turning point is reached, there the Holy Spirit leads Him to the place of temptation. The contest between light and darkness reaches a new climax. Here was light neither overcome by nor diffused in the darkness – but light only. The experience of Jesus at His baptism was precisely this, that the Holy Spirit confirmed in Him this conviction that He was God's Son. To be the Son was to be like one whom the Father had created. In being called God's Son He is distinguished from the rest of creation. This is a new beginning and He is the first-born among many brethren who will follow after Him. And all who will thus follow will also be born of the Holy Spirit, for Jesus wil continue to conduct the Holy Spirit into other lives. As the ancient creed has it, 'the Holy Spirit proceeds from the Father and the Son'. Thus can be seen the meaning of the saying in St John's Gospel, that there the Holy Spirit was not given until Jesus was glorified. The act of the Holy Spirit is conceiving the new man Jesus was not completed when He was born nor when He was baptised nor through His ministry, but when He was raised from the dead. The resurrection took place by the power of the Spirit.

The glory of the cross is that the darkness did its worst and light triumphed. Jesus became the author of light for all men and for the world; not only light Himself but He through whom men come to the light. What St John affirms is that way in which the work and witness of the Holy Spirit are dependent on this light that streams from that cross.

The affirmation 'conceived by the Holy Ghost' is followed by 'born of the Virgin Mary'. The word 'born' is a purely human word and underlines the fact of Jesus as man. There certainly was the question as to who Jesus was, but there was no question as to what He was. He was a man. His identity, as God incarnate, as Christ and Messiah, as the Son of God and Son of Man did not mean that in any sense He was only a kind of appearance – God appearing as a human being, a theophany or an avatar. Divinity and humanity are not mutually exclusive, making necessary a conjunctive relationship between them. Jesus is not God and man, but God-with-man made man.

The new beginning which is promised in Jesus Christ is thus a new beginning within reach of men's humanity. In being born anew to a new life in God in Christ, men do not cease to be what their natural birth makes them. Jesus was conceived by the Holy Spirit and was born man. Those who are re-born by the Holy Spirit, and become men in Christ, remain men. The new is embedded in the old and remains within it in the source and powers of its renewal.

The word 'born' however is joined to the phrase 'of the Virgin Mary'. At the time the Creed was formulated, there was the Christian community's grateful recognition of the woman in whose womb Jesus was conceived and by whom He was born. It is almost impossible to trace the tradition of the virginity of Mary back to this source, but the thrust of the phrase itself is not so much to say something about Mary as it is to say something about Jesus. Mary denotes the point of human history at which the incarnation happened and the mention of her name re-emphasizes the meaning of the word 'born'. Jesus arrives on the human scene in the one way in which all men arrive – born of woman. In St Peter's speech announcing the Christian news, there is no mention of Mary, not is she part of the Church's proclamation anywhere in the New Testament. Indeed, it is this silence concerning Mary as a virgin in the preaching of the Church which makes one believe that 'the Virgin Birth' could not have been invented. Had it been invented for polemic or apologetic purposes, it would have been used for those purposes. Besides, the Lukan and Matthean birth stories cannot be swept aside. Why was Mary's answer to the announcement that she was to be the mother of the Christ so like the prayer of Jesus at Gethsemane: 'Let it be to me according to your word'? Had she a cross to bear because she bore a Son when she was still a virgin? Did people ever point to her and say that she was a mother out of wedlock? We read how the scribes and pharisees said to Jesus in their controversy with Him, 'We were not born of fornication'.

The argument which raises questions as to the possibility or necessity of the Virgin birth is pointless. The simple issue is what happened and whether there is sufficient evidence to believe that this is what happened. One thing is certain. In the Church's teaching, the identity of Jesus is never made dependent on His being born of a virgin. If He was born of a virgin, it was not because the incarnation was dependent on a virgin birth. Then why? Can it be that the virgin birth was the means by which Mary received her revelation as to who her Son was? It was God's sign to her, given to uphold her in all that happened to her Son. As the record puts it, 'Mary kept all these things, pondering them in her heart'.

Suffered under Pontius Pilate
Crucified, dead, buried

In the Creed , there are two names associated with Jesus – Mary His mother and Pontius Pilate. The name Pontius Pilate identified and describes the historical circumstances of Jesus. Pontius Pilate was a representative of the milieu, humanly speaking, under which Jesus lived. The verb 'suffered' is a comprehensive verb. He endured the circumstances of human living. He chose to identify himself with the joys and sorrows of those among whom He lived. He so put himself at the mercy of men in order to serve them that they were able to reject Him. And when the crisis came, He accepted Pilate's authority to pass judgement on Him.

The verb 'suffered' pinpoints the fact that the life He lived was lived for others. He had no profession or occupation which was His own. He was not even a Rabbi with a school of learners. His life was like seed sown into the furrows of life; there to die. To put it very simply, He was a man behaving as God would have a man behave in the midst of other men. 'Suffered' is the right verb to use to describe such a life.

He was crucified. The word 'crucified' conveys very much more than simply the manner of His death. It explains why He died. He was crucified because secular power found in Him a revolutionary. He was crucified because ecclesiastical power adjudged Him a blasphemer. He was crucified because the common people found Him awkward.

In reading the gospel story, it is impossible to escape the conclusion that His death was something which He himself accomplished. 'The death which He was to accomplish in Jerusalem', are the very words of the gospel narrative. During the last days of His ministry, He kept out of the way when He found that there were plans to assassinate Him. He came to Jerusalem for the Passover because that was the time He chose to precipitate the crisis. He kept the initiative to the last in His own hand. Even Judas received permission from Him to do what He did. In Gethsemane, Jesus says to His captors, 'You arrest me only because I am willing to be arrested'. To Pilate He says, 'You would have no power over me except as it is given to you by God.' 'I lay down my life of myself. No one takes it from me', were His words to His disciples. In other words, it was His will that His crucifixion be accomplished. He was born of woman and lived a human life. He began His ministry by receiving the baptism of repentance for the remission of sins. Having identified Himself with sinners, He became, throughout His ministry, part of the lives of ordinary men and women. He showed inexorable concern for those who became His enemies. He showed deep understanding for those who were the outcasts of society. Prostitutes and publicans were often in His company. On the Mount of Transfiguration, He accepted the burden of accomplishing His death. In the Garden of Gethsemane, He submitted to His Father's will that He become what sin makes man become. So He died a felon's death, identified as a man on whom rested the curse of God. He who became man became what sinful men become. So that He cried, 'My God! My God! why have you forsaken me?'

When Jesus cried from the cross and said, 'It is finished', He was declaring that the deed was done. The incarnation was completed. Faith in God had been maintained against every assault of temptation. God's faithfulness to man had been demonstrated in spite of every form of human rejection. And finally, death itself was entered into and conquered. Death took Jesus captive but was unable to hold Him. His life was so completely the life of God that death could not hold Him. All men die. Some die protesting. Some die with resignation. Some die in triumph. Jesus died in agony. There was a quality in His death which revealed death for what it was. The sting of death, says St Paul, is sin. When Jesus died, it was that sting that He wrested and which He finally plucked out. He made His captor captive. When Jesus died, death too was finished. He made possible by His death and resurrection a life beyond death available on earth as present experience and continued beyond death as glorious reality.

At the heart of the Christian faith is the affirmation that Jesus is Saviour. How He saves has been a subject of theological discussion across the centuries. But the Christian faith is not anchored to any particular answer to the question how. It insists only and simply that it is He who saves. Jesus does for men something they cannot do for themselves. He creates a hatred of sin and a desire for an amendment of life. He gives the grace to repent and the faith to appropriate forgiveness. He establishes the relationship with God as Father and maintains the constant acknowledgement of that relationship. He lays claim to a man's life and, when it is offered to Him, fills it with meaning, so that it works for Him and with Him in the work of salvation in which He is engaged. Finally, when life's day is done, a man dies in the Lord even as he has been enabled to live in the Lord.

Jesus suffered. He was crucified. He died. The Creed goes on to say He was buried. This last item of man's earthly story too is part of His story. His body knew the grave.

In the affirmation that Jesus died and was buried, there is also the intention to say what needs to be said if the rest of the story is to make sense. Because of the Christian claim that Jesus rose from the dead, theories were advanced, some of which denied that He was given separate burial. In the gospel narrative itself, it is said that those who crucified Jesus set afloat the story that the disciples of Jesus stole His body from the tomb. Another current story was that Jesus did not actually die, but only swooned on the cross and revived later. Gnostic speculation about Jesus as a theophany could not admit that the theophany could die. Against all their suggestions, the affirmation is quietly but deliberately made, that Jesus died.

The general custom with the bodies of crucified men was that they were thrown into a common grave. The gospels however give a circumstantial account of the burial of the body of Jesus. The names of those who buried Him are given. The story is told how they got permission to bury Him and where He was buried. It is impossible to evade the conclusion that here is a record of what actually happened. A rejection of the truth of the record is possible only on the ground that the gospel writers were deliberately lying.

The Christian Creed affirms quietly, but strikes firmly, the basic notes of a completely human life – conceived, born, suffered, crucified, died, buried. The meaning of it all is more than the human imagination can conceive. But it was a human life that was lived. It was in and through a human life that God's deed of salvation for all men was wrought.

Descended into Hades:
the third day he rose again

The phrase 'descended into Hades' means that He went where the dead go. It emphasizes the fact that Jesus actually died. It is useless to argue the question whether the word 'descended' is an appropriate word to use and whether it correctly describes what happened. The point is that it is intended to convey a theological truth. It says that God entered into man's experience of death and man's situation beyond death. God became man, not only among the living, but among the dead.

St Paul makes use of the words 'descended' and 'ascended' to express the thought that all of creation is filled with the presence of Jesus. There is no place or circumstance in which Jesus is not available and active as Lord. Neither the dead nor the living are outside the consequences of the incarnation.

Then follows the phrase 'rose again'. At this point in the Creed the sphere of human history is transcended. The resurrection of Jesus is not simply something that happened to Jesus. It is also something that happened to death. Death is the boundary of human existence. Those on earth are on this side of death and those who have died are on that side of death. In Jesus, this boundary has been breached, so that in Him they that are His and remain inseparably one. Death cannot separate them. When it it said therefore that He rose on the third day, what is being said is that from the historical end the resurrection was attested from the third day. His disciples saw Him buried on Friday and met Him alive on Sunday.

This gap between Friday and Saturday has no reference to Jesus in Hades. By the resurrection the affirmation is made that Jesus is with men always and all the time whether they be on earth or in Hades. He is always with the living and the dead. It is because this is true, that it is possible not only to live in the Lord but also to die in the Lord. Sometimes and quite unthinkingly the phrase 'descended into Hades' is swept aside as if it were mythology. The picture behind the phrase is certainly old-world, but the truth it contains is of tremendous significance. 'He rose from the dead.' Therefore, life on earth and life beyond death belong together in an inclusive relationship. In a real sense, because Jesus is risen death is no more.

When Jesus was crucified, those who plotted that act simply intended to get rid of Him from living in their midst. He troubled their consciences, challenged their prejudices, upset their structures and was generally proving himself a nuisance. When it is said that Jesus rose from the dead, what is meant is precisely this, that those who killed Jesus did not achieve their objective. He came back to live among men and do for all men and to all men, what He did for those and to those among whom He lived in the flesh.

To talk about immortality is to talk about the continuance of life beyond death. To talk about the resurrection is to talk about the conquest of death. Jesus is everyman's contemporary. The census of the world is always one short. They forget to count Him. The testimony to the resurrection of Jesus which is found in the New Testament is a testimony to this fact about Him. The form this testimony takes is the form of a record which speaks of an empty tomb and resurrection experiences. The emphasis falls on the different ways in which men and women met the risen Christ. He was known and recognized in person-to-person encounter. They met Him as He made the word of scripture luminous to them. They knew who He was in the breaking of bread. They experienced His presence in the way in which He delivered them from fear when He came to them behind closed doors. They knew His compulsion through the gift of the Holy Spirit. He was there when they had nothing to show for their toil. He was there when they were hungry at the breaking of day. St Paul would add, 'Where sin abounded grace did much more abound' – He was there to waylay the sinner and to save him.

As one reads the preaching of the Apostles, one is

struck by their insistence on the resurrection of Jesus as something which happened to Him and not merely to them. He rose from the dead and appeared to His disciples. But whereas His appearances are part of the testimony, there is no reference in apostolic preaching to the empty tomb. To put the matter directly, the apostles do not seem to have wanted to prove that Jesus rose from the dead. If they had wanted to do this, the empty tomb would have been central to their argument. What they wanted to do rather was to invite men to meet the risen Christ, hence the emphasis on the ways in which they met Him and He met them.

The silence concerning the empty tomb in relation to the resurrection of Jesus is comparable to the silence concerning the virgin birth in relation to His incarnation. These were private signs. The one was a sign to Mary, the other was a sign to the first band of apostles. The nature and idiom of the biblical testimony to the resurrection of Jesus are determined by its intention. Its intention is to become a medium through which the living Jesus may confront those who hear the testimony. It is of the nature of a lightning-conductor. When a lightning-conductor is set up, it becomes also a testimony on the fact that there is such a thing as lightning and to the expectation that lightning will fall. The resurrection narratives of Jesus are of the same kind. Properly read, they become the medium through which the risen Christ is encountered in power.

There is a further implication in the affirmation that Jesus Christ is risen from the dead. It means that just as death is experienced throughout life, in sickness, sorrow and suffering, so is the resurrection. The power of the risen Christ is immediately available for men in actual living. It is available as a conquest over sickness, sorrow and suffering and is a victory within them and in spite of them. This power is available also as power over sin and temptation. The path to goodness is not created out of moral endeavour on man's part, but this endeavour is self-created by the incursion into human life of the power of the risen Christ. In other words, the resurrection of Christ is the guarantee and sign of man's ultimate future, a future however which is already present experience.

It is unnecessary to say that, if this is what Easter faith is about, the questions which should be posed in understanding it are in the last analysis neither questions of history nor of science. The lightning falls when and where it wills. The proof of the resurrection is the proof of those places and persons, where it can be shown that the lightning fell. It is these lightning-conductors and the way the lightning fell which are described in the original gospel narratives of the resurrection. It is no good looking at a lightning-conductor and asking for proof of the lightning. In what manner and under what guise the risen Christ will come to any man, we cannot pre-determine. But since He is risen, He will come. The truth of the lightning-conductor is the lightning.

A man attested by God:
But you acted in ignorance
'Jesus of Nazareth was a man attested by God by miracles and deeds which were amazing demonstrations of divine power in action.' The life of Jesus was such that His contemporaries found themselves constantly alerted by it. God was, as it were, pointing them to Jesus all the time, and saying to them, 'Look at Him'. Hence the point that St Peter makes in his speech when he says, 'God was acting through Him and you, men of Israel, saw it'. Nothing was done in a corner. Everything was out in the open. There was no beating of

103

drums, but neither was that life lived so quietly as to go unobserved. And yet, the point is made that it was in ignorance that the men of Israel who sent Jesus to His death did what they did. They failed to understand why Jesus so disturbed them, so they simply removed Him as they would eliminate any other disturbance. They killed the Prince of life, but they did not know that it was the Prince of life whom they killed. They thought that they were simply getting rid of an upstart carpenter.

The authority under which and by which Jesus was crucified was that of Caesar. However, Pilate too did not know what he was doing. As St Peter puts it, 'He had no knowledge of the law of God'. The Jews who handed Jesus over to Pilate were ignorant of who Jesus was. Pilate did not even have the means of knowing who Jesus was. He was a Roman and not a Jew, and the scriptures were a closed book to him.

Now, says St Peter, it is a new situation. Jesus has been raised from the dead and exalted to the right hand of God; and there are witnesses all around bearing testimony to who Jesus is and what His life and death means. It is no more the time of ignorance. So then, says St Peter to his audience, 'Repent and turn to God'. They can now see what in them caused their ignorance and why they could not recognize Jesus, so that they can turn to God in repentance asking Him so to change them that they can become men who would gladly accept Jesus.

Crucial to the invitation to repent is the new situation created by the existence of the Church's witness. There is now the possibility of seeing from within a believing community what only such a community can point out. 'God spoke to you through the life of Jesus. He attested it. Yet, you did not understand. Now listen again, for God is speaking to you through the same life with which you have not finished and will never finish. For His life did not end in death. It was not possible that He should remain under death's control.'

'We have personal knowledge and can personally guarantee', says St Peter, 'that God resurrected Jesus from the dead.' It is this personal knowledge that is at the heart of the believing community and to that knowledge that St Peter invites his hearers. They must meet the risen Christ just as St Peter and his companions had met Him. Of this meeting they will come by repentance. It is, as it were, the whole life of Jesus with His death and resurrection that is made the context within which people stand when the total story with its meaning is proclaimed. When they stand here, they have been taken out of the time of ignorance and planted in the now which belongs to the day of salvation. The dividing line between the time of ignorance and this now is the news proclaimed. How can they believe, says St Paul, without a preacher? What the preacher does is not only to bring them the news but to move them into a new situation in which, hearing what the believing community believes, faith is made possible for them also.

When Jesus was crucified, He prayed, 'Father, forgive them, for they know not what they do'. This prayer cannot mean that because of their ignorance they should be judged not guilty. Nor can it mean that they should not be punished for what they did. Forgiveness may or may not involve remission of punishment, but it always does involve the call to repent, so that reconciliation may be effected. God must be reconciled with guilty men. The prayer of Jesus was answered when God offered to those for whom Jesus prayed the gift of reconciliation with Him. That the Jesus they rejected and crucified is now alive meant that they could turn to Him in repentance and faith, while the believing

105

community, whose witness to Him they heard, offered them through that news the means of repentance.

St Peter having said, 'You acted in ignorance', goes on to make a further explanatory affirmation. 'This was God's way', he says, 'of fulfilling everything which He foretold through the prophets, that the Messiah should suffer.' What happened, happened, because that was the nature of things. Scripture makes clear what human nature is really like and how it will react to God's demands.

Scripture also makes clear what God is really like in His dealings with men. God is so unchanging in His purpose, and pursues them so persistently, that again and again it is the same pattern which is traced out in the encounter between God and man. The Messiah necessarily fits into this scriptural foreshadowing. The foretelling which is in scripture is not prediction. It is the way in which the story of the relation between God's design and man's disorder is told. The relation between God's faithfulness and man's unfaith is traced so that the inner compulsions of history are made explicit and the ways of God with men are explained. What happened in and to Jesus was as if a recurrent theme suddenly burst into full song and what was present as allusion and suggestion suddenly became specific and concrete. Those who worked their will on Jesus were ignorant of the real import of what they were doing, while those who believed in Jesus saw in them the instruments by which scripture was coming to its fulfilment. Now the call comes that those who rejected Jesus should repent, because even if they were ignorant, they did what they did deliberately. Therefore, they must become the kind of men who would accept that what they did was wrong. The very fulfilment of scripture, of which they had been the instruments, demanded this repentance.

The question addressed to St Peter at the conclusion of his speech was, 'What shall we do?' St Peter's answer is plainly put, 'Repent, become members of the community of faith, accept forgiveness from Jesus Christ for what you have done, and be prepared to participate in His risen and on-going life through the Holy Spirit.'

Proclamation of the good news in Christ and its consequent call to repentance are the true context of the testament of faith. The Creed is not concerned with facts to be recorded but with lives to be changed. How often the point is missed, that it is because of and within the witness and witnessing life of the Church that the articles of the Creed make sense. They are not just facts to be recited. They are always within the context of the double assertion: what you did you did in ignorance, now repent.

And ascended to heaven
and sits at the right hand of God the Father

The resurrection of Christ is an event which can be viewed historically, even though the central substance of what is affirmed is more than historical in nature. But the word 'ascended' which follows is not historical at all. The risen Christ is not time bound and it is of the risen Christ that it is said that He ascended into Heaven.

When one reads the gospel records, what one finds is that there was a period after the resurrection of Christ during which He appeared and disappeared in such a way that His disciples soon discovered that He was always there, even when they did not see Him. Once this lesson was learnt, the truth about the presence of the risen Christ could be stated from the other end. He lives in heaven. This is obviously picture-language. But the meaning is clear. Jesus is beyond space and time. He is bound by neither. He is always here because He is already there. His final promise was, 'Lo, I am with you always, even unto the end of the world'. The experience of this promise is the proof that He has ascended to heaven.

Let not the symbolism of the words 'descended' and 'ascended' be allowed to mislead. He who fills the depths, fills also the heights. He whose presence with man is guaranteed by the resurrection is also He whose otherness to man is asserted by the ascension. Jesus cannot be domesticated within the human story. He is God-with-man become man. He is God-with-man as God.

In the gospels, Jesus is reported as having said more than once that all authority was His and that the Father had given Him this authority. When the Creed says that He sits at the right hand of God the Father, it is this fact about His authority which is being affirmed. Human life is lived under the authority of Immanuel. Jesus is the heart and content of God as Immanuel. It is not possible to understand man's life on earth in any other terms but this. It is Jesus born in humiliation, suffering in obedience, crucified through rejection, under whose Lordship men live. The nature of this Lordship is revealed through the resurrection. Men are free to enact a Calvary. But they do not have the power to prevent the resurrection. Christ's Lordship allows for the cross, but not for the cross to be the last word.

There naturally is a desire of men for the intervention in their lives of a God who is not thus weak and strong at the same time. But there is no satisfaction that way. True living demands that one trusts God, both when God is revealed in weakness and when He is revealed in strength. The exhilaration of the Christian life lies in knowing Him crucified as well as knowing Him risen. The ultimate truth, the truth which is at the seat of authority. He who is at the right hand of the Father, is Jesus Christ. He is the truth by which life has to be lived and by which it is governed.

Seated, will come to judge

The Creed follows up its affirmation of Christ's ascension with the statement 'sitteth at the right hand of God the Father'. Here is obvious picture language, but the meaning is clear. The Creed asserts what is said about Jesus many times over in the gospels that all authority belongs to Him, because it has been given to Him by the Father. The ruler and architect of human history is Jesus Christ. The method of His rule is the cross. He remains so much at man's mercy because He loves them that they can reject Him. But while men can enact the cross, they cannot prevent the resurrection. He is Lord. The New Testament faith carries forward this assertion of Christ's present sovereignty into the further assertion that He will come again. He came once in humiliation. He will come again in glory. He came the first time to initiate. He will come again to consummate. When He came in the flesh He came to share man's life, to suffer for him and to die. When he comes again as risen and ascended Lord, He will come to bring the human story to its end. He will come to judge.

The judgement of Christ is not a simple exercise in deciding between right and wrong. It is not the final awarding of rewards and punishments. It is not just a question of salvation or damnation.

The judgement of Christ is to bring each human story and the total human story under His leadership, so that the true import and value of everything is tested and that which stands the test is all brought into a fullness which is beyond everything that we can ask or think. We bring our lives to Him as timber and marble and

109

stone are brought to the builder. That which is of poor quality has to be set aside. But there will never be one lost good. Everything that can be redeemed will be redeemed, everything that can be used will be used. The judgement is not the judgement of a law court. It is the culmination of an enterprise. The old creation grows until the new creation is revealed. The old man dies that the new man may be born. We are saved but as by fire.

And then beyond judgement lies the Father's Kingdom. The Kingdom of the cross is transformed into the Kingdom of glory. And the prayer of the ages is answered – 'Our Father, Thy Kingdom come'.

CHAPTER FIVE

I Rejoice in the Holy Spirit

JESUS keeps God safe for men : The Holy Spirit makes Jesus available for all men. He takes all men to Jesus Christ and produces many sons of obedience.

Through him I know God as Father, for I recognize Jesus Christ as the first born of many brethren. Christ becomes my deed of inheritance, for I learn to confess Jesus Christ through the Spirit.

Jesus is Lord, but He becomes my own Saviour. He is Judge of all men, but He is my peculiar possession through the Spirit. All men are for Jesus Christ, but He is given to me.

I realize what I am, through the spirit. I long for what I shall be, because of the Spirit. I rejoice, for I am already in the Spirit.

When one reads the Gospel records one is struck over and over by the humour and joy of Jesus. Jesus was an intensely happy man. Someone gives two reasons to show that Jesus was a happy man. He was constantly invited to weddings and feasts. No one invites an unhappy or grumpy man to a feast. He will ruin the party. Jesus always radiated joy. Also little children took to him. According to psychologists children sense emotions. They do not easily take to people who are unhappy in their lives.

Christian life can be characterised only as a life of joy. One of the experiences of the Spirit described in the early Church is of people being caught up in a state of ecstasy. They lost all sense of time and reason and their human tongues were loosened to ecstatic utterances. But the Christian experience of joy is not just a sudden emotional outburst of bliss. It runs deeper into the very foundations of the Christian faith itself. Just before Jesus faces the last gruelling days of His earthly life, He tells His disciples, 'These things I have spoken to you, that my joy may be in you, and that your joy may be full' (John 15:11). It is an inexplicable joy, for it was joy in the midst of, and in spite of, sorrow and tragedy. Even the possibility of death did not rob life of its joyous meaning. St Paul, who was a prisoner for the Lord, still writes, 'Rejoice in the Lord always; again I say rejoice' (Philippians 4:4).

To say 'I rejoice' is as much a testament of faith as to say 'I believe' or 'I confess'. The joy is the joy of finding sonship and the result of living as a son.

Some people are often burdened with the sense of their moral life; others with the sense of their religious life. 'Thou shalt not' is the signboard written large over many, often all, areas of life. Life becomes fear; fear to walk lest we should fall. The fear of guilt in the presence of the law is intolerable. In fact we can take the opposite example of St Paul, the pharisee of the pharisees; one who, under the law, was blameless. All that the law demanded he had done. But still he needed God the Father of our Lord Jesus Christ. He was still outside the good news. He knew the law and had kept the law, but what he needed was God's love. He needed the love of the Father.

The elder son, the son of the law, was still outside his inheritance. His quarrel with his father was that all that was demanded of him he had done. But still the fatted calf was not his. The startling revelation that comes to him is, 'All that is mine is yours' (Luke 15:31). He did not have to earn his inheritance. It was already his. He had only to ask for it.

When my brother and I were children, I remember we used to ask our mother the things we wanted from father. Her reply always was, 'Go and ask him'. He was father. The father participates in the love and joy of the children and they in turn in his. The asking is within the total relationship. The attitude of the son of the law is as one who stays at home but is still away from home. He does not participate fully in the love of the father. I remember the trips made by my father abroad when we were little children. He used to ask us before he left what we would like to have when he returned. We used to ask him for all kinds of things. We ourselves knew that half of what we asked we would not get. But the whole point of his being father was that we could ask freely without any inhibitions. Asking was part of, and an expression of, the bond of love between us. But whenever he asked our servant, he got always the same reply, 'I will accept whatever the master gives.' He had not entered the inheritance. The inheritance was not his to ask freely. It had to be earned. It was also an expression of the distance between the master and the servant. The master was not the father. They were not part of an intimate fellowship.

Many Christians say, 'We are prepared to receive whatever God gives. He gives out of his wisdom and love.' This is not enough. The whole point of a father is that we are free to ask. Later we learn to ask for the right sort of thing. At the same time we are free to ask for anything, because the burden of discrimination is not on us. He knows what is good for us. I rejoice because I am free. He bears my responsibility.

113

The father's present is an expression of love and not a reward for service rendered. The fellowship and understanding is more than a sum total of gifts. It is more than the just refusal or giving of a gift. We understood that we often received, not because we deserved it, or even asked for it, but because he loved us. But what is more important is that we were often refused, not because we did not deserve it, but because there was a greater plan or reason. At this point the father's responsibility for me turns into my participation with him.

The difference between the son of the law and the son of the promise is that the son of the promise knows what the father is doing, while the son of the law does not. 'No longer do I call you servants, for the servant does not know what his master is doing; but I have called you friends, for all that I have heard from my father I have made known to you' (John 15:15). The servant carries out orders. The son participates.

Another way of stating this is to say that both asking and receiving are parts of the same relationship. Asking is an expression of trust; receiving is an expression of response. The sin in the Garden of Eden is where the father gave but the son refused to receive. The Father gave what was good and he also decided what was evil and therefore should not be given. The son refused to receive what his father considered was good for him. Since the son refused to respond to the father's love by receiving, now he must accept the father's love by asking for it. He knows that we love him when we ask; 'Ask, and it will be given you; seek, and you will find; knock, and it will be opened to you' (Matthew 7:7). God has gone the full length and given us even His only begotten Son. Now the initiative is on our side. We must show appreciation by receiving and asking for this gift. To justify in terms of work is still to maintain the inheritance outside the promised land. The gift is free if only we will take it.

I rejoice in the Holy Spirit, for I know the Father is mine as He has given me the Son and I have received Him. I know the inheritance is mine because He gives me and takes me to the Father through Jesus Christ. The Spirit teaches me to receive Him. The Spirit also makes me ask for Him. I am safe, for He is my response and my obedience.

His Power

'Do not hold me, . . . I am ascending to my Father and your Father, to my God and your God' (John 20 : 17).

'Truly, truly, I say to you, he who believes in me will also do the works that I do; and greater works than these will he do, because I go to the Father (John 14 : 12).

When Jesus was on earth, he was limited. He was limited by His body. His work was limited by evil forces that kept battling against Him. But once He ascended to the Father His work becomes even greater and He works even more powerfully, for now He is outside the powers of evil and he is no longer limited by an earthly body. He is in the presence of God. Often we wish to limit Jesus. We want to cling on to Him and possess Him. If we would only let Him go and let Him work in a larger dimension than our own needs and parochial self-interests, then we would see how wonderfully in a new way all things fall into place. We become part of a larger design.

The Jews thought that they had finished with Jesus. The disciples thought that they had lost Jesus. But He arrives even more powerfully in His Church, His new body.

We cannot limit God. Jesus tells Nicodemus, 'The wind blows where it wills, and you hear the sound of it, but you do not know where it comes or wither it goes; so it is with everyone who is born of the Spirit' (John 3:8). The wind bows where it wills. We can feel it but we do not know from where it comes and where it goes. But there is one thing that we can do, and that is to stand in the wind – catch the wind squarely in our faces. What Jesus is asking Nicodemus to do is to join the enterprise.

There is John the Baptist doing something. Here is a church that is doing something. There is a school or hospital that is working. We have to be involved. People are afraid to be involved. It may demand too much and we may end up with more than we bargained for. Is it not true that every time the church thinks of an advance, the first thing it does it to plan 'a retreat' – or the next conference? We feel content to stay in a room with all the doors and windows shut, just circulating hot air. Even an electric fan is not enough. Let's keep the doors and windows open and, even more, stand out in the breeze. Nicodemus came for a consultation, a retreat, and the reply he gets is 'stand out in the wind'.

But the Spirit is more than a breeze or a gentle wind. He is the *desert* wind. He is a storm. He uproots everything in His path. Our fears are justified. It is dangerous to be caught in His tracks. But when we are caught by Him, there is also the exhilaration and the joy of being carried on the wings of the air. It is not we who are the actors; it is He who carries us and places us where He wills.

There is this fact also. The splinters that are carried by the storm from some already-created wreck, can in turn cause a lot of damage. We are crushed by Him and then we are hurled by Him. A lot of damage in the wake of a storm is caused by these splinters that can smash into people and things. We must become victims

116

of the storm. Then we become powerful weapons in his hands to use as He wills.

'For our Gospel came to you not only in word, but also in power, and in the Holy Spirit and with full conviction. You know what kind of men we proved to be among you for your sake. And you become imitators of us and of the Lord. ... (Thessalonians 11:5,6a). It sounds like arrogance, but the early apostles were worthy of imitation. They had become victims and in turn a source of damage. The Spirit was infectious. The church of Thessalonica had in turn become caught by the Spirit through the early witnesses. It is convincing, because they themselves had become victims.

We can feel the wind. Nicodemus felt the wind. But even more than that, the wind must get hold of us. There are three ways of being the witnesses of an event. 'An illustration will make this clear. Suppose there has been a car accident. I can be a witness, because I saw the accident. I happened to be on the road at the time and saw the accident happen. I am a witness, because I was a spectator. I can also be a witness if I was in the car when the accident took place. I escaped unhurt, though perhaps badly shaken, but I can testify to what happened. I am a witness, because I was involved. I can also be a witness to the accident if, in the accident I was the person injured. I would then in myself be proof that an accident took place. I am a witness, because I was the victim.'[1]

We become evidences of his power, not by controlling or possessing that power, but by becoming controlled and possessed by that power. The church does not possess the Spirit, but rather the Spirit possesses the church. The Samaritan woman asks whether it is to be Samaria or Jerusalem. Jesus' reply is that it is neither

1. Daniel T. Niles, *The Context in Which we Preach*, The second Annual John Knox House Lecture, July 6th, 1956.

Samaria nor Jerusalem (John 4 : 21).

One of my professors jokingly pointed out that in the list given in 1 Corinthians 2:28 the people that came practically at the bottom of the list are the administrators. But today the people that come at the top of anything are the administrators. They are the most powerful and the most important category. They keep order. But the early church was accused of disorder, of turning everything upside down. The Spirit cannot be institutionalized.

Was this not the sin of Simon? (Acts 8 : 18ff). He wanted to domesticate the Spirit. His power does not belong to the prophets only. He does not belong only to kings. He belongs to everybody simply because He has chosen to outpower Himself on all. His overpowering of us is our salvation as well as our danger.

The Greek word used for disciple means not only a scholar of books, it means also an apprentice who is learning a trade. The problem is that we always remain the apprentices, but this is also our redemption. He is the master craftsman. We think we are fashioning a piece of wood, but we find that He is already fashioning us. What we fashion will be in turn a measure of how we are being fashioned. Our image will be reflected on our work. The question is to what extent our image is the reflection of God's image.

We must preach about the liberation and also bear witness to this power. As we do this, we will also find something happening to us and our work. It is not our working but the Lord's. We are upheld by Him and the success of our ministry and even our salvation is not dependent or conditioned by what we do. He has already done it.

'For we are his workmanship, created in Christ for good works, which God prepared beforehand, that we should walk in them' (Ephesians 2 : 10).

His Assurance

'We have this as a sure and steadfast anchor of the soul, a hope that enters into the inner shrine behind the curtain, where Jesus has gone as a forerunner on our behalf, having become a High Priest for ever after the order of Melchizedek' (Hebrews 6 : 19-20).

'If the Spirit of Him who raised Jesus from the dead dwells in you He who raised Christ Jesus from the dead will give life to your mortal bodies also through His Spirit who dwells in you' (Romans 8 : 11).

The curtain or veil in the Christian sense has a double meaning. There is the veil of the temple which separates the presence of God from His people. There is also the veil of death which separates God from His creation. But now the altar of the temple is in the midst of the congregation where we break bread and drink wine in the presence of the Lord. In Christ, God's presence is brought into the midst of men. At the same time we stretch out our hands in the dark beyond death and find that it is held, held by Him beyond the veil as we are anchored and grounded in Him who is our hope. Thus it is a hope that is not yet seen, but it is a hope that is sure, for it shall be revealed.

In our Tamil Bible, the word used for hope when literally translated means, 'that faith which is worth believing'. It is that faith which is worthy of belief. In the human sense, to hope means there is the element of doubt. It may not happen, but we hope that it will happen. In the Christian sense we know that it will happen, for it has already happened. Therefore the author of the epistle to the Hebrews is able to say, 'Now faith is the assurance of things hoped for, the conviction of things not seen' (Hebrews 11 : 1).

The assurance that it has happened and will happen

119

is the work of the Spirit. In St Paul's eighth chapter to the Romans, which is a great chapter on the work of the Spirit, he states that Christ was raised by the Father through the Spirit and if we have His Spirit we shall also be raised like Christ, '. . . we ourselves, we have the first fruits of the Spirit, groan inwardly as we wait for adoption as sons the redemption of our bodies' (Romans 8 : 23).

We are running a race which shall not be futile or in vain, because death is not the last answer which robs life of its meaning. Christ is the pioneer and we follow in His footsteps. His triumph beyond death shall also be ours. But it is not only triumph beyond death, but the destruction of death itself – the redemption of our bodies. We shall discuss the resurrection in another section, all we need to bear in mind is that the Christian faith and witness is not about a heaven or place beyond death, where we shall live for ever more, but rather about a new creation here on earth. We are the first fruits of that new creation and we shall inherit this earth when the Father returns. 'Thy Kingdom come' is the Christian's prayer. The last enemy to be destroyed is death and then the Father shall be all in all.

It is more than sheer accident that Jesus should be raised from the dead on the first day of the week and that the Spirit should also descend on the first day of the week. It is not the Sabbath, but the first day of the week. The new creation has begun, but the Sabbath is yet to be. There is a finish and an end, for Pentecost is the completion of the harvest. But still it is just the first fruits to be resown, which must die. It is finished, because Christ is risen, but it is not finished, for we must die.

The assurance is sure, for the purpose is greater than ourselves. 'For the whole creation itself waits with eager longing for the revealing of the sons of God' (Cf.

Romans 8:19). It is as though the resurrection of Christ is our hope, but at the same time our resurrection shall be the hope of all creation. We dare not fail, for the redemption of creation itself depends on us, but on the other hand we cannot fail, for our 'yes' and 'no' is interwoven into a pattern that is larger than ourselves. As the Spirit was at work in the first creation, He is at work in His new creation. When our faith begins to sag, let us look at Christ who was perfected by the Spirit. When our strength begins to fail, let us remember that we have to meet an obligation that is larger than ourselves. We cannot fail God's creation.

The dawning of the new age is pointed to by Jesus in His earthly ministry itself. In the ninth chapter of John, we have the incident of the man born blind. The disciples were interested in a philosophical discourse as to how and why he was blind. The man was bound and they wanted to know the nature of the bondage. Jesus was not interested in that. He was interested in what could be done. 'We must work the works of Him who sent me while it is day; night comes, when no one can work' (John 9:4). The works of God are made manifest in him, in that he received his sight. There is sin and there is bondage. The reality of sin has relevance only as far as it is dealt with, and can be dealt with, by God.

In turn, His presence is given to His church. The first instalments of the promise that He would be with them was experienced by the disciples during Jesus' earthly ministry itself. Jesus commissions His disciples and gives them power and authority. All that they had to do was to exercise it. The first thing to remember is that we have the power or we do not have it. It has nothing to do with the faith of the recipient. The lame man at the temple gate (cf Acts 3:1f) was only asking for alms. He did not ask for healing, but he was healed. Jesus

121

says this bluntly in the story of the boy with the epileptic fits. 'Then the disciples came to Jesus privately and said, 'Why could we not cast it out?'' He said to them, "Because of your little faith"' (Matthew 17:19b). His presence is with us and this is His assurance. All that we need to do is to exercise His authority. Our schools and hospitals have a distinct function to perform. They are exercising Christ's authority in the liberation from sickness, superstition and other bondage. To say that healing and education are free is to confuse the issue. God's gifts are indeed free. He sends the rain on the just and the unjust. But the question is whether we know that God is sending the rain. Jesus healed the lepers, but only one saw the miracle. He saw Christ's presence and His power and returned to give thanks. The question is whether we see God at work. If so, we must point to the source of the authority.

The point of faith in the recipient is just this; he does not need faith to receive healing. He needs faith to discern the giver. Healing is not the end; rather, wholeness is the end. Healing miracles are also opportunities that Jesus uses to set up personal contacts with the recipients. They must come to know him for His own sake and He must come to know them. The woman with the issue of blood must be known. She needed more than physical health. She regained herself. When we know the giver, the converse is equally true. We need not stipulate the particular form of the gift. The gift is just a measure of the giver. Jesus in fact was not interested in healing for its own sake. Peter comes and tells Jesus that people are waiting for Him, and His reply is that He must preach in the other villages also (Mark 1:35f). The assurance is that the Spirit helps us to see the Lord's work. As He witnessed and completed Christ's work, He will also complete ours.

His Guarantees

Faith is partially based on the record of deeds already done. Our life is grounded and built on this. Our assurance is that this is so. But still, what is the guarantee that we are not just shadow boxing, with no real target before us? (cf. Corinthians 9:26). Our guarantee is that the Spirit has set our sights on the real target.

It is also possible to preach without believing. The objective reality must also become subjective experience. The Spirit makes us say 'Amen'. He makes us say that this is so. Therefore faith is a gift. Faith is created by the Holy Spirit that we may receive what God has already done. He also helps us to discern and participate in what God is doing. It is not by ourselves, but He working in us, 'bringeth all things to completion'. 'For it is not the man who commends himself that is accepted, but the man whom the Lord commends' (2 Corinthians 10:18).

'It is God who establishes us with you in Christ, and has commissioned us; he has put his seal upon us and given us His Spirit in our hearts as a guarantee' 2 Cor. :21, 22). God must give what He demands. God Himself creates the response that is demanded of us and at the same time gives us the proper form of address that is required of us. He is 'Abba, Father!' (cf. Rom. 8:15b).

We know the proper form of address, because we know in whom we have believed. He is not father in a general sense, but in the specific sense of being the Father of our Lord Jesus Christ. The earlier promises of God saw their fulfilment in that He kept faith with His people. When we think of God, the only way in which we know Him is by seeing His acts of faithfulness, kindness and mercy to His people. They knew the God who was dealing with them and with whom they had to reckon. But now the story becomes even more specific. It is the God who kept faith with His own son. The only way to know God is to see Him and His ways as He dealt with His own son.

This world often seems meaningless. There looks to be no purpose or plan. There is death, violence and pain. Evil often seems to triumph. Motives and goals are misunderstood. But still this is not the end, either for myself or for the world. He is my Father, who is also the Father of our Lord Jesus Christ. This is His world that we are talking about. The priestly writer affirms that God is good in his record of the creation story. But it is the goodness of God that is affirmed in the midst of, and in spite of, the way of suffering that the people endured in exile.

It does not stop there. God is able to do what He does, because He also creates our response through the Spirit. He keeps and shapes our obedience. The picture that we see is not one where God only was faithful, but where His son was also kept faithful and obedient to the Father to the very end. Therefore the Father also raised Him up, having kept faith with His Son who had been perfected in obedience. It was not that Jesus rose from the dead. According to the narratives, He was raised from the dead, raised by the Father. Therefore if we are children of the same Father, 'then (we are) heirs, heirs of God and fellow heirs with Christ, provided we suffer with Him in order that we may also be glorified with him' (Romans 8:17). What is demanded of us is nothing less and nothing more than the obedience of Jesus Christ, which ended on a cross.

The Spirit gives me my address. I know to whom I belong. He creates my end, for He gives my response. But He is also the centre of my life, for He frames my prayers. We do not know how to pray and we do not

124

know what to ask. He teaches us to pray and, even more than that, He prays for us. 'Likewise the Spirit helps us in our weakness; for we do not know how to pray as we ought, but the Spirit himself intercedes for us with sighs too deep for words' (Romans 8:26). It is for this reason that we also find the admonition, 'Do not grieve the Holy Spirit of God, in whom you were sealed for the day of redemption' (Ephesians 4:30).

Christian living is simple. It is living in the Spirit. He prays for us and His prayers are always answered. The reason our prayers are not answered is that they are not the prayers of the Spirit for us. Christian religion is equally simple. It is the theology as to why it is so, that is difficult to rationalize. The problem is that most people have made their theology too simple and made their religion difficult with superstitious fears, rituals and candles. All that we need to do is to rest in the Spirit and let the Spirit be the articulation of our lives.

Once I was listening to someone preach on a text of Thessalonians 1:7 – 'Pray constantly'. Before long I found that the preacher was asking us to 'work constantly'. Prayer is not primarily work, but simply an attitude. It is an attitude of waiting upon God in all circumstances of life. Prayer is the tuning in of our lives to God's mission in us, for us and by us.

'The Kingdom of God is as if a man should scatter seed upon the ground, and should sleep and rise night and day, and the seed should sprout and grow, he knows not how . . .' (Mark 4:26f). All that the man did was to sleep. It is rest and restfulness in God. Our anxious and busy work may only be the bruising of the fruits of the Spirit. He who does not gather with Him will only scatter. Prayer is always our 'Amen' to God. Prayer is often not petition but glorification. It is not asking God for something, but rather answering Him.

'(In Him you also) . . . were sealed with the promised

125

Holy Spirit, which is the guarantee of our inheritance until we acquire possession of it, to the praise of His glory' (Ephesians 1:14). There is no cause for anxiety, for He is our guarantee that we are on the right track. He creates our obedience. He frames and articulates our prayers. We know we shall be obedient sons, for He has already come and taken possession of us. The Pauline writings address the Christians over and over again as the 'saints'. They are not yet saints, but they will be saints, for God is Holy and those in His will become what he wants them to be. The nature and work of God can qualify His people, for His Spirit has already arrived.

The wheat must be separated from the tares. But further, the good wheat must be separated from the chaff. 'Simon, Simon, behold Satan demanded to have you, that he might sift you like wheat ... (Luke 22:31). For it was fitting that he for whom and by whom all things exist, in bringing many sons to glory, should make the pioneer of their salvation perfect through suffering' (Hebrews 2:10). He makes Christ what He is in order that we may become what we should be. The guarantee that we will not be chaff is ultimately based on His work. The prayers that Christ prayed for us and is praying for us are also responded to by the Holy Spirit from within us.

One of the root ideas in Greek for the word guarantee, translates itself as an 'engagement ring'. We know the marriage will take place, because we are already engaged. The Bridegroom is assured of the faithfulness of the Bride, because of the Spirit which is keeping her faithful. We are able to say 'Amen' in the Spirit. At the same time, through the Spirit we know that the Bridegroom is sure, for all the promises of God find their 'yes' in Him (cf 2 Corrinthians 1:20).

His Teaching

'According to the scriptures' is the confession of the early Church. But which scriptures? It is only by the knowledge and guidance of the Holy Spirit that we see that the way Jesus took is in accordance with what Jesus taught and that this in turn is what was expected of Israel by God. It is not that the Old Testament interprets Jesus Christ for us, but rather that Jesus Christ interprets the Old Testament for us.

The Spirit teaches us all things and brings them to our remembrance. In turn He makes us witnesses not only of what we have, but also of the re-enactment in our own lives what happened. In John 13:34 we have the picture of an impotent man (Peter) as he seeks to keep the commandments. But 'you cannot lay down your life for me now. But you will afterwards. You cannot follow me now, but you shall follow afterward'. 'I do as the Father has commanded me, so that the world may know that I love the Father' (John 14:31).

What is tested is Christ's sonship and ours. At baptism, the testimony of the Spirit is, 'This is my beloved Son, in whom I am well pleased'. I am God's son. But then, how am I God's son? The Holy Spirit drives him into the wilderness to think this out. It is not enough to know; we must also so live that we are aware of its implications. There was the Principal of a school. His son was the student of the same school. As the Principal's son, he took a lot of liberties, he used to break the rules of the school, he refused to obey the teachers and the Student's Council, and he bullied the other students. He was the Principal's son. I am God's son, but then I must live accordingly. Regarding Jesus' life, the author to the Hebrews writes, 'Although he was a son, he learned obedience through what he suffered' (Hebrews 5:8).

'If you are the son,' is the temptation of the devil. But he gives no new answer to the problem. The problem of man is that, from the very beginning, he has rejected the father's bread and has been trying to turn stones into bread by tilling the soil, by hard toil and labour. 'In the sweat of your face you shall eat bread' (Genesis 3:19). What Jesus, as God's son, discovers, is that all this toil through anxiety is not necessary. 'Do not be anxious about your life, what you shall eat or what you shall drink, nor about your body, what you shall put on. Is not life more than food, and the body more than clothing?' (Matthew 6:25.) Why do you distrust God? Why do you think He will give you a stone if you ask for bread? 'What Father among you, if his son asks for bread, will give him a stone? Or if he asks for a fish, will give him a serpent?' (Matthew 7:9–10). The temptation in the Garden of Eden was exactly this. Man in his anxiety refused to trust the goodness of God. He created us and therefore knows us. But man refuses his wisdom and love. 'No, I must know good and evil. I must know for myself!' This is even the problem today. The counsel of the older generation is rejected. 'We are the modern generation. We know and even if we do not know we shall still learn by our experience.'

There is the possibility of sonship outside the Garden of Eden. But what Jesus says is that God is enough and that what He gives is sufficient. Since we have lost the Father's presence, we waste time on the wrong road and the wrong problems. The gentiles also receive the bread from the Father. Therefore Jesus goes on to say that even more than for the bread we should ask for the Holy Spirit' 'If you then, who are evil, know how to give good gifts to your children, how much more will your heavenly father give the Holy Spirit to those who ask Him' (Luke 11:13). It is He who helps to discern

128

the presence of the Father. He is our true nourishment. The present without the presence is meaningless. At Christmas time, we receive presents from our loved ones, but what we long for even more is their presence. If we have them, that is enough. God is enough. He will provide the bread.

There is a prayer which is always answered immediately, the prayer for the Holy Spirit. Without Him we cannot begin the Christian life. For some prayers the answer is 'yes'. For other prayers the answer is 'no'. Still for other prayers the answer can be, 'not yet'. But the prayer to God for the Holy Spirit is always answered with a 'yes'.

'Not bread alone, but the word of God', says Jesus. The temptation that the early Church faced was also the same. 'It is not right that we should give up preaching the word of God to serve tables' (Acts 6:2b). The temptation that the Church faces is to become another social institution that simply doles out bread. In our preoccupation with the bread, the presence can be missed. The second temptation puts this in a concrete form. How do we know that God's presence is enough. What is our security? We often wonder whether God's presence is with us. God's presence provides its own rainment for the lilies of the field. When we force the issue, we often end, not with God's glory, but with self-glorification. We are asked by the devil to so live for God that we have the praise of men. We say that God has done this and done that, but our emphasis remains upon ourselves. We take the centre of the stage. We must let God deal with His church. Other attempts and methods to make the Church acceptable have also to contend with the risk of losing His presence. Jesus did not seek His own glory. 'I say as the Father has bidden me' (John 12:50b). He reflected God's glory to the extent of His own personal rejection and crucifi-

129

xion. When we are turned towards Him, we reflect His glory, and that is our covering. If we withdraw from Him, or should He withdraw from us, then we need new covering. They who had lost God's presence needed the fig leaves to cover themselves.

The third temptation concerns the concrete relationship between the present and the presence. We can have the world as a gift, but the world is truly mine only in the way God chooses to give it to me. I cannot make it mine even in His own name. Jesus rejected the political Messiahnists and Zealots of old. The Church is called today to wrestle with the problem of political programmes and what political parties have to offer.

Having discovered His identity, His sonship, Jesus is led to the Mount of Transfiguration. The Spirit had witnessed and taught Him in the wilderness. The new answers must be grounded in God alone. He must go through the crucifixion and find that He is enough. All men are brought to the Mount of Transfiguration. It is the height of glory outside the Garden of Eden.

There is the possibility of power and authority and the exercising of sonship without realizing the way of the Father. The crucifixion can be evaded. The temptation was, 'If thou art the son, use your power'. Jesus says, 'All authority and power is in my hands', but this is after the crucifixion and after He knows the true way of the Father by obedience and trust.

The Christian pilgrimage is a cyclical process. We move with the agony of the cross before us and then find the joy of triumph when the cross is behind us.

Jesus says, 'Ask for the Holy Spirit'. But the Church often does not seem to need an advocate, for she misses her vocation and has no crucifixion to face, no case to be tried nor judgement to be faced.

His Fellowship

'When the Spirit of truth comes, he will guide you into all the truth.... All that the Father has is mine; therefore I said that he will take what is mine and declare it to you' (John 16:12–15).

The test of the Son before the crucifixion was whether He was glorifying Himself or His Father. The event of Pentecost is where the Holy Spirit does not glorify Himself but the Son. What we have is where the Son glorifies the Father and the Holy Spirit glorifies the Son or where the Father glorifies the Son and the Son in turn glorifies the power of the Spirit. The essential fact is that very rarely does each person point to Himself. It is always the concern with the will of the other. This is true fellowship where each is upheld by the other.

This should be the pointer to the way of Christian fellowship. The essential witness of the Son to the Spirit and the Spirit to the Son is seen in a small measure in the miracles that Jesus performed. They were witnesses to the breaking in and power of a new age. They are signs of the new creation where all old bondages are broken-sicknesses of the mind, body and spirit. In Matthew 12:22f, we have the instance where Jesus' authority and power is questioned. His power is ascribed to the devil. Jesus' answer is revealing. '... But if it is by the Spirit of God that I cast out demons then the Kingdom of God has come upon you.... Therefore every sin and blasphemy will be forgiven ... but the blasphemy against the Spirit will not be forgiven. Whoever says a word against the Son of Man will be forgiven, but whoever speaks against the Holy Spirit will not be forgiven ...' (Matthew 12:28–32). This could be illustrated with a human parallel. Paul writes to the

Galatians, 'My little children, with whom I am again in travail until Christ be formed in you' (Galatians 4:19). What Paul is saying in short is, 'If you reject Christ, also bear in mind that you are rejecting me and my teaching. My work among you is in vain'. To reject the Son of Man is to reject the Spirit, for it is He who is in travail within us, pointing us to Christ. Humanly speaking it is possible to say that we did not recognize Christ in human flesh, but then, what about the witness of the Spirit who is trying to break the hardness of our hearts and is guiding our thinking into the truth concerning the Son of Man? To deny the Son means that we are sinning against the Holy Spirit. Also at the same time this is a foretaste of the power of the Spirit. This is His work to come that is already being performed by Christ.

But then there was the other side, where men tried to control the Spirit and even tried to use the Spirit for their own self glorification. Personality cult is a constant temptation. Like the anti-Christ, there is also the anti-Spirit! Even those who say that they have the Spirit could actually be working against the Holy Spirit. Really to know whether it is the work of the Holy Spirit, is to see whether the person is witnessing to Christ – 'No one can say Jesus is "Lord" except by the Holy Spirit' (Corinthians 12:3). The person who acts should not be a distraction or obstruction but should rather stand alongside and point to the source. Paul again asks, 'Was Paul crucified for you? (1 Corinthians 1:13). Paul is not important. He points to Christ. To put it another way, 'When people look at you, will they be able to say that Christ died for you?' Others seem more important than Christ in your lives, including Paul. To make sure that we are pointing to Christ, we must all see that we do not come between a person's faith and his relationship to Christ.

We must make sure, too, that we are not letting some-body else come between us and our witness to Christ. I remember my father saying, 'We need no character cer-tificate from any man. When we go on the other side, all our character certificates are only to be filed and left behind'. We are not working for the praise and glory of men. He is our judge. He must justify. The same pattern should follow within the life of the Church. "Now there are varieties of gifts, but the same Spirit . . . to each is given the manifestation of the Spirit for the common good' (1 Corinthians 12:4–7). The problem in our Church is not only where those claiming special gifts are so lost in speaking about their own gifts that they often end, not in glorifying Christ or the Spirit, but themselves, but also where they cast doubt on the validity of other ministers and their ministries. We must be able to stand by one another and justify each other's work. It is not that one person by a special gift has a mark of favour, but that he has been given that gift to use for the whole fellowship. Also all talents and gifts are equally important. We need and use each other's gifts for the Lord. He justifies our work, and even more than pointing to each other's ministries we all point to Christ.

When we know that God is our covering and that He is our security, then we can stop worrying about human praise and get on to something else. That is, our con-cern for other men. They also are those for whom Christ died. Each man has his worth before God be-cause all men are created in His image, and further-more Christ died for each of them. 'We (now) regard no one from a human point of view . . .' (2 Corinthians 5:16). Christ died for you and that is enough for me. I am not interested in what other people say about you or think about you. You may be a child or you may be a grown man. You may be a saint or you may be a rogue. What man says about you does not count. But then there is the other side. We cannot stop where we are. We have to grow into mature manhood in Him, to the extent that we become like Him. That is, 'I decided to know nothing about you except Jesus Christ and Him crucified' (I Corinthians 2:2). Christ is our pattern. It is not enough to be just God's children; we must become like Christ. 'When He appears we shall be like Him' (1 John 3:2). That is the goal.

The fellowship is where we are slow to defend our own rights, but where we are quick to defend another man's rights. But of course, it breaks down where the other does not do the same for me. Paul to the Galatians reminds them of this. There was a time when the Galatians would have even given their own eyes to Paul (cf. Galatians 4:12f). But now he was suspect and his ministry was suspect. He had fully given himself to them and become one of them, but now he faced personal rejection. This is the price that we must pay in the same way that Christ paid. To make ourselves popular we cannot preach something else. Ultimately it is His fellowship and we must guard His sheep for Him. But this can also be a way of finding out whether it is 'His fellowship' or 'my fellowship'. In a human fellowship or association I choose friends who think like me. My rejection could also point to the fact that this is His fellowship. His ways need not be my ways.

The fellowship is given. We do not create it, but discover it. Also, how could we possibly say that we love God, when we are unable to love the person next to us who is also God's son given to us (1 John 4:20). The members of the family are given. My brothers and sisters are given. I can find my friends. I am born into the fellowship and my relationships are already bound.

His Guidance and His Mission

The importance of the Holy Spirit as the guardian of the Church who has taken the place of Christ in the flesh is pointed to in the narrative of the Holy Spirit being given to Samaria (Acts 8:14). It is of significance that baptism in the name of the Lord Jesus Himself is not enough. They must receive the Holy Spirit. The Baptism of John the Baptist is also not enough (Acts 19:2). The question raised in both cases is, 'Have you received the Holy Spirit?' In fact, the whole of the Acts of the Apostles has been characterized as the Acts of the Holy Spirit. There is His guidance at the councils of the early Church, in the setting apart and laying on of hands, in the individual guidance to people like Philip at the incident of the Ethiopian eunuch and in the case of Paul who is forbidden to enter Asia. He was present in the convincing of hearers at the proclamation of the word. But we have singled out three places as of importance in the life and ordering of the church.

To speak of the Spirit's guidance primarily means to point to the places where He is at work, the places of His presence. When we think of Christ and ask where His presence is assured and where He is really present, three definite places spring to my mind, that are based on His promises. He is present where two or three are gathered together in His name. He is present in the dominical sacraments of the Lord's supper and baptism. He is present in the midst of the worshipping congregation which is His body where the word is proclaimed.

When we think of the Spirit also, we could single out three places which definitely point to His presence. There is His arrival in time which was His incarnation at the constituting of the early church which was Jew-

135

ish. Once again we have to take note of the Spirit when He descended on Cornelius and his household – the gift to the gentile church. The third place is His presence with the church in times of persecution (Acts 4:31).

When the spirit descends on the Apostles, His presence is pointed to by the cloven tongues of fire and the rushing of a mighty wind and the speaking of tongues. They were the physical accompaniments of His incarnation. The best way to describe this event is to say that this was the descent of the Spirit in the flesh in the same way that Christ was born in the flesh. To ask again for the same signs in the daily living of the Church is not necessary. He has descended and He abides with His church. We need not test or ask for further signs. To ask for the physical descent of the Spirit again is like asking that Christ be born in the flesh again. The event has already taken place. The spirit manifests Himself in a physical form through His descent when and where it is necesary as special guidance to the Church. Just because a person like Sadhu Sundar Singh had a Vision of Christ, it does not necessarily follow that all Christians must have a Vision of Christ. We believe in the events as they are recorded and as they did happen. The spirit as the dove or the cloven tongues of fire has already given Himself to the Church.

There is the problem of speaking in tongues in relation to the Spirit's manifestation and guidance. The problem is with us from the very beginning. The reception of the first three thousand at the day of Pentecost itself is not followed with the speaking of tongues. Also, the problem is made no less easy by the fact that the audience on the day of Pentecost were devout Jews. 'Now there were dwelling in Jerusalem Jews – devout men from every nation under heaven' (Acts 2:5). There-

136

fore the question springs to mind, why the speaking in different languages, when they were all Jews of the dispersion who had come together for the feast at Jerusalem. Surely they should all have known their mother tongue. It is not that the Apostles spoke in different languages, but that the hearers heard of the conviction of the Word, each in His own language, the language of his experience. Someone is explaining a problem to a hearer, but he is making no headway. In spite of all explanations, the other does not understand. But then, suddenly, there is the exclamation, 'Now you are talking! Now you are speaking in my own language.' There is the language of ecstasy, of exuberance in the Spirit, but this language has to be translated and communicated into conviction, which is also done by the Spirit to the hearer.

There is also the different interpretation that has to be reckoned with, which is given by Paul. 'For one who speaks in a tongue speaks not to men but to God: for no one understands him, but he utters mysteries in the Spirit' (1 Corinthians 14:2). Therefore he says, 'He who speaks in a tongue should pray for the power to interpret' (1 Corinthians 14:12). Even more than the gift of tongues, what Peter had at the day of Pentecost was the ability to interpret. When people accused the Apostles of being drunk he was able to tell them what was happening. He was able to discern the ways of God. But the greatest interpreter is the Holy Spirit Himself. He convinces the hearer.

What Paul says is that what the Church needs is the power to preach, or to prophecy (cf. 1 Corinthians 14:1). 'To prophesy' means, not to foretell, but to discern or rather speak about the nature of God with clarity. The reason why the things that the prophets said came true many a time was not because they foretold the future correctly, but because they knew their

God and realised how He would act in a given situation.

The speaking in tongues is a mystical ecstatic experience and the language remains unknown or misunderstood till it is interpreted. Preaching is partly the ability to interpret and help people to see and use their gifts in a creative way. A private experience has to be made to grow into a public form of worship. Otherwise speaking in tongues, like any other gift, can only lead to confusion and dissension in the Church. 'For God is not a God of confusion but a God of peace' (1 Corinthians 14:33). Praying at home is one thing and praying at public worship is a different thing. Speaking in tongues as a private experience is one thing and to make it come into play in the edification of the total community is a different thing.

Speaking in tongues is just one of many gifts. It is one of the gifts of the Spirit (1 Corinthians 12:7-11) (cf. Ephesians 4:11). The important thing that is mentioned in both references is that all these gifts should be used for the edification and the building up of the Church. The speaking in tongues becomes an experience of edification only when it is interpreted. The gift of discernment is needed and is given to help the Church build one another up and to work together for the common good.

But the gift of discernment is also needed at another point. It is needed to help us see the working of the Holy Spirit, outside the Church. This is clear in the second incident. The Spirit cannot be contained in the Church where the Church is made to move on a set of rails that have been laid. Peter is in fact taken off his guard when he finds that Cornelius and his household had already received the Spirit before he thought of baptizing them. In fact, that was the defense to the council later. 'What could I do? They had already received the Spirit. I could only baptize them into the church' (cf. Acts 15:7b). Peter was able to interpret this event at Cornelius's house correctly and was also helped to discern the Spirit's movements by the prior vision about the clean and unclean food (cf. Acts 10:10).

The first time Peter faces a non-Jewish audience with the dilemma of whether they should be counted within the Church or not, is at the house of Cornelius. (This is also additional evidence to show that those who were baptized at the day of Pentecost were only Jews. He needed to be prepared by the vision and had to see the gift of the Spirit being given to the gentiles before he was prepared to baptize them.) The problem is also solved for him. The Spirit accepts them even before Peter can raise problems concerning the proper forms of acceptance laid down in the traditional institutional Church. We find Philip caught in a similar predicament when the eunuch inquires of him – 'See, here is water. What is to prevent my being baptized?' It is as though the eunuch took the initiative and made Philip baptize him. Philip was taken off his guard.

We also have to watch for the Guidance of the Spirit and His presence in signs and tokens that He is performing outside the organised life of the Church. He brings the new harvest. The problem is that we are so used to giving, so used to taking the initiative, that we are often unable to receive. The incident comes to my mind, where one of my friends had gone for a consultation involving the Harijans (depressed classes or the untouchables). My friend said that the whole discussion centred around the Christians telling the Harijans, 'If you want to join us, it is all right, but we are not prepared to give our daughters in marriage to you'. The leader of the Harijans smiled and replied, 'You need not give your daughters. All that we are asking is

139

that you accept us. Just receive us.' My friend said, 'Suddenly it dawned on me as to what our Christian Mission was doing. We are constantly thinking in terms of what we can give. We gave our schools, we gave our hospitals. We gave, gave and gave. Now suddenly we are faced with the problem of receiving and we do not know what to receive and how to receive.'

The third instance is the assurance of His presence in our time of trial and need. He who was present at our Lord's baptism is present at the birth of the Church. He who was present with our Lord at the transfiguration and the following events of His mission is present with us in our hour of need. The point at which we are ultimately tested to see whether we are of the Spirit or not is at a time of crisis. What we are tested about is our life in the Spirit. What we need to show is not the gifts of the Spirit, but the fruits of Christian living (cf. Galatians 5 : 22). To find out whether we have the Spirit or not we often judge in terms of the gifts of the Spirit. But the gifts must bear fruit. The Church has also to remember that its primary business is to feed the flock. The wheat and the tares will grow together. Let them grow. Both are fed with the same food. God sends his rain on the just and the unjust. It is not for us to judge whether a person is of the Spirit or not. He will separate the wheat and the tares. But may be we would have an indication towards the end of a man's life as to whether he has abided in the Spirit or not. Conversion is the beginning of the Christian life. We still have to grow and bear fruit. There is a vast difference between receiving the gifts and so building these gifts into us that they become the work of the Spirit which abides. Let love be the aim, rather than speaking in tongues. Let edification be the aim, rather than a private experience.

The Holy Spirit reaps the harvest. The Church is asked to garner the grain and help in the resowing. We should not let any grain go to waste. At the same time we must help all grains to bear fruit. But above all we must keep our eyes open for those places where the descent of the Spirit takes place through special signs of break-through in the life and pattern of the new community that He is forming. At these junctures the speaking in tongues is not a private experience it becomes a community act of life and witness. The events of Pentecost, Cornelius's household and times of persecution were more than private experiences. They were places where the Spirit descended and lived with His people.

CHAPTER SIX

We live by His gifts

JESUS took the way of the Father. The cross He encountered was not incidental but volitional. Today people speak of their illness as crosses. Some would even say, 'My wife is my cross'. These are burdens and not crosses. The cross is met at the point of personal rejection where the Son of Man stands rejected by all men. The cross is the result of the opposition caused by Jesus because He obeyed the will of the Father and refused to compromise with the ways and gifts of men.

Men give us gifts when they like us. When we are rejected by men we are still not alone, for God provides His gifts. The Holy Spirit creates and provides for us the council of faith. The last section of the creed is not a miscellaneous assortment of things which do not fit anywhere else, but are the definite acts of the spirit. God gives us the Spirit and He is our companion on the journey. He also provides us His gifts from the Father and the Son.

We live by His gifts

Life is an answer to what we do with God's gifts. He provides for everyone. The problem is that man responds to what God gives in different ways. Some are aware of His gifts and accept them with grateful thanks. Others accept it as a matter of course. It is God's business to provide. Others know from where it comes but are in open rebellion. There are others who are ignorant of the fact that they are fed by the same Father and have to be shown the way. There is also the attitude of the servant who lives by the justice of his master. He obeys the will of God, but does not know Him as Father.

The essential thing to recognise is that we are fed by Him whether we like it or not, whether we acknowledge it or do not acknowledge it. When St Paul speaks to the Athenians, it is to this truth that he seeks to point. What he says is, 'You say it is to the God who is unknown. We do not know this God. But you know this God even as your prophets say, 'in Him we live and move and have our being".' The problem is that we know this God, but not fully. What Paul seeks to do is to set out this God in the light they had so far known and groped for in a distant way. Paul begins with their experience and shows them that though they did not fully realize it, it was this God who had brought them so far. They must know fully before they can acknowledge. They are still in a sense in a state of ignorance.

This is life's experience. A mother feeds her infant baby. The baby does not know that it is fed by its mother. If the baby says, 'I will drink the milk only after I know', the baby will be dead. If the mother says, 'I will feed the baby only after it knows', she will not be the mother. The mother feeds the baby and the time does come when the baby is able to say, she is my mother who has fed and brought me this far in my life.

But when the Apostles speak to the Jews, their whole tone and attitude changes. This is the God whom we know. It is He who has led you out of bondage, therefore repent. Stephen is especially severe when he also refers to them as the stiff-necked people. The time of ignorance is over for all men, but especially the Jews, who have no excuse at all. They already know.

People must know before they can repent. We must so present the gospel that they are able to see Jesus at work in their own lives. Otherwise, the whole emphasis on reptenance is meaningless. Repentance is a possibility only when they know whom they have wronged, whose gifts they have rejected. Those of us who say 'We know' find that the judgement is even more severe because knowing, we have done nothing about it and in many ways have crucified the Son of Man.

The hope of the Christian gospel lies in the fact that ultimately man is redeemed by God's acts. Repentance itself is a gift wrought in our hearts by the work of the Holy Spirit. One of the prayers of the early Church was 'Come, Holy Spirit, come, ... convict, convert, consecrate, till we are wholly thine'. He prepares us and also gives us.

The joy of life in the Holy Spirit leads to the Discovery of belonging. I rejoice, we live. No sooner is one caught up in the Spirit than he discovers he belongs to a family. It is a joint inheritance. There are only two sins which are unforgivable. One concerns the Spirit as He seeks to bring us into obedience to the person of Christ. 'Therefore I tell you, every sin and blasphemy against the Spirit will not be forgiven' Matthew 12:31). The other is as He makes us belong to the fellowship of His family. 'For if you forgive men their trespasses, your heavenly Father also will forgive you but if you do not forgive men their trespasses neither will your Father forgive your trespasses' (Matthew 6:14, 15). The problem is not that God cuts us off, but that we cut ourselves from His family. It is foolish for me to leave my brother outside and go to my father and say, 'I rejoice in your presence, rejoice with me that I am here'. The father's joy will not be full till the brother, whom I have left outside also returns. On the other hand, it is equally foolish to go to the father's house and to expect that the brother whom I hate will not be there, for he is equally my father's son. To live with the father means also that I live with my brother. I think I have got rid of my brother on earth, but discover when I arrive he is already there in my father's house to greet me. Heaven is a place of surprises.

When people give us gifts, these gifts call for certain decisions and new adjustments. If you give a lady a gift of a sari, you cause the problem for her of finding a suitable blouse to match it. If you give a man a tie, he has to find socks to match it. If you give someone a motor car, he has to build a garage. If you give someone an elephant, you will probably ruin him. When Christ comes into our lives, there are changes. First of all, He throws out all that is unnecessary. Dr T. Z. Koo gives the example of empty space. The important thing in a building or vessel is its empty space. The architect is always worried about the wastage of space. If we fill a house with furniture, there will be no space left for us to live. A cup may be exquisitely fashioned, but if it has no hollow space for the water, the cup is useless. When Jesus comes into our lives, He creates the empty spaces and the Holy Spirit brings about the reordering of what Christ provides. Chaos is the result of the rebellious man. It is also the result of the pressure of the gospel. Our lives are emptied but are also filled.

We are often worn down by the cares of the world and our responsibility. The surprise of the gospel is in that what we strive for is already done. We live by His gifts. In many homes we find a verse that is hung prominently. It reads 'Christ is the Head of this house, the unseen guest at every meal, the silent listener to every conversation'. We begin by saying that Christ is the Head and then go on to speak of Him as our guest. He is the host of every meal and He provides for His disciples as He presides at the table. The disciples on the road to Emmaus invite Christ as their guest. He blesses and breaks the bread. They know him as their Lord.

The biblical picture is the picture of the wedding feast. We shall be invited to the supper of the Lamb, He breaks the bread and distributes the wine. His toil is our bread and His blood is our life. But the person who attends the wedding feast is one who has already participated in the normal life of that home. A person who has had no connection with that family does not invite himself to the wedding feast nor is he invited. There are many Christians who attend the Lord's supper once a month or once a year. For the rest of the year they are absent in the worshipping life of the congregation. This is like attending the feast without visiting the home. Of course, the Christian gospel is where everybody is invited to the wedding feast. But then we could turn up without the wedding garment (cf. Matthew 22:11).

Humanly speaking, when we give a gift to a person, what we mean through the gesture is that we are giving ourselves to that person. When a person rejects a gift, what it means is that we are rejected ourselves and when a person accepts a gift, what it means is that we are accepted. But when it comes to God, though we take and use His gifts, it does not necessarily follow that we accept Him.

The Holy Catholic and Apostolic Church

There are two movements pointed to by this confession. There is the movement towards God and there is the movement towards the world. There are two words Holy and Church that describe the action from the Godward side and there are two words Apostolic and Catholic – that describe the nature of the engagement with the world. The problem is that the very meaning of the word 'Church' has changed. The church is composed of those who 'belong to the Lord'. They are those who are 'called forth' or 'called out' and remain as the people of God. Its description has to come from the Godward side but most modern descriptions tend to define the Church from patterns taken from the world. The Church is in and for the world, but it is not of the world. The engagement with the world has to be 'Apostolic'. St John says, 'Jesus, knowing that the Father had given all things into His hands, and that he had come from God and was going to God, rose from supper, laid aside his garments and girded himself with a towel (John 13:3, 4). Our work in the world can have true perspective only when we are clear in our own minds as to whom we have come from and to whom we are returning. There are certain intransigencies set in the midst of the engagement itself. We cannot use any methods we like. Jesus took the road that ended on the cross. He took the road that was set by the Father and which ran against the grain of all human understanding. We come from Him and return to Him.

The reality of the world has to be affirmed, but only as it finds its new reality within the purpose of God. Jesus spoke of making disciples of all nations as the task of the Church. The relation between the Church and the world is seen here. We are not asked just to create disciples by separating people from the world, but by making these people so live that they disciple the world itself. The Church is holy because God is holy. The description is adjectival. This is confessed

147

by the Church so living that the world is pressurised and discipled into living as God the Father of our Lord Jesus Christ wants the world to be. There is always a tension between the Church and the world. Thus the word Apostolic has a double reference. The Church is from God, but this aspect is discovered and only understood as the church lives out its mission in the world.

The word that explains the world as it should be seen in the context of God's mission is 'catholic'. It is the world in its wholeness. To speak of reconciliation is to speak of wholeness. What we see is a fragmental world. The world must be made whole. The Church as the new community, the new world to be, prides itself of its catholic nature. Whatever be the shortcomings of the Church's life, when the Church claims to be Catholic, what it is speaking about is the nature of the world as it ought to be, and naturally the church should first be able to show this catholicity in its own life. Our Christian churches and institutions took certain stands on issues facing the world and now these have in a sense permeated society and been absorbed by it. The lump is being leavened. But then, the bread has yet to be turned out.

Discipling and catholicity go together. The degree of health and wholeness of the world is dependent on its response to its origin as God wants the world to be. There are various things that subject the world to false ends. There are various points of false integration that give a measure of stability, peace and security. All these have to be dealt with. Paul gives a list of things (cf. Romans 8:38, Ephesians 3:10) that are part of the created order, but which now hold sway over man. They are all creations. But now the eternal plan and purpose of God is revealed. The demonic nature of creation becomes visible in the same way as the pride of man becomes visible when man and the world assert themselves over against God. The main problem is that good things are pressed in to the service of the bad and furthermore there are forces which are subtle. Paul speaks of principalities. Principalities are the result of sin being wedged into social structures. To follow fashion is a good thing, but there are lots of things that go in the name of fashions and modelling that are unspeakable.

There are two dimensions to life. There is the vertical dimension, where man and the world face God, and there is the horizontal dimension, where men face each other as they organise the world to meet their needs. There is the fear of the loss of identity. The gregarious nature of man seeks refuge in group thinking and patterns. This produces its own peculiar problem of isolation and insulation. Groups are set in competition over against each other. On the other side we find the loss of identity caused by the fragmentation and atomization of society, whereby individual man can become an anonymity. We end with the chicken and the egg puzzle where all the faults of men are blamed on the environment and the society, and in turn all the social ills are blamed on the nature of man.

The Apostolic mission of the Church is to try to get the vertical and horizontal dimensions constantly to face each other. There are the human attempts at reconciliation, or rather experiments in community living. These end in a city that is a babble of voices. There is also the city that comes down from heaven (Revelation 21:26) whose builder and maker is God (Hebrews 11:10). There is also God's way of reconciliation.

Today the main slogan is about 'the brotherhood of man'. 'The Fatherhood of God' does not lead to the brotherhood of man, but to the 'Family of man'. Today my own father is dead, but we of the family are still brothers. There is the brotherhood. But when he was alive it was more than a brotherhood. We were a family. He was the centre of our lives and the one point of integration. God is alive and creates a family. The nature of the fellowship and the brotherhood is dependant on Him who is the head. Therefore the church constantly faces the paradox between man's activity and God's design and vice versa. 'In the year king Uzziah died I (also) saw the Lord' (Isaiah 6:1), is the vision of Isaiah. The king is dead and the days of prosperity for the kingdom seems to be over. The holiness of God, His presence, is felt in the midst of a human dead end. In a time of calamity a young girl brings forth a child and has the hope and faith to still name that child 'Immanuel'. All things seem to point in the direction where there seems to be no God, but still the girl says, 'There is God; He is with us'. The earth is also the Lord's. The Church is also the Lord's. Therefore in all situations we can also see the 'Lord'.

There was the debate in our church about making Sunday a working day. There were those who said, 'Let us hand over this day to the government'. The point that needs to be realized is that the day is not ours, but the Lord's. It is not for us to hand it over or even to keep it. But what we see, having passed through that whole debate and government planning, is that we 'also' saw the Lord. There are many of those who were against the move, who are now saying, 'The church attendance is better after Sunday became a working day'.

The holiness of the church is its hope as well as its danger. The 'wholeness' of the world is also its hope as well as its danger. The end is not the world in rebellion to God, but the world where God is King.

The Communion of Saints

To say that one believes in the communion of saints is to confess to an experience that we live at three levels. At the same time these three levels criss-cross one another. Firstly, it is the experience of the heritage into which we are born. Secondly, this is to say that the links between the living and the dead are not cut at death, but that we can still meet and possess the dead. Thirdly, it speaks of a life beyond death in which we also participate by faith.

To speak about the heritage of the saints is to know God's dealings with men through the generations. Isaiah says, 'Hearken to me, you who pursue deliverance, you who seek the Lord; look to the rock from which you were hewn, and to the quarry from which you were digged' (Isaiah 51:1). We must know the pit from which we are dug. Our life has a history preceding it. Our life also shall have a history following it. We have responsibility towards those who have lived before us and also towards those who shall live after us. Life is a baton race. We pick up the baton from him who has run before us and we must also so run that he who comes after us is prepared to pick up the baton from us. This means that those who come after us should think it worth while to continue the race which we have begun. It also means that we must prepare the future generation and get them ready for the race that lies before them. 'Therefore,' writes the author to the Hebrews, 'since we are surrounded by so great a cloud of witnesses, let us also lay aside every weight and sin which clings so closely, and let us run with perseverance the race that is set before us' (Hebrews 12:1). It is as though our forefathers, having run their race, are now part of that crowd of witnesses who

151

are cheering us as we run the lap that lies before us.

Traditions become ours only when we seek to meet and live with those who have lived before us. Every time we use our set orders of worship, we are speaking about the communion of saints. We have entered their world and they have entered ours as we worship our one common Lord – that is, at the time we begin to stop speaking about the greatness and pride of our heritage in terms of famous ancestors, and rather begin to speak about their God and ours. Traditions become the vehicles through which we meet our common Lord. Traditions are symbolic. they also mediate God's presence. The Bible is a history of men shaped and recorded as the deeds of God. God is the primary actor in the drama. When Jesus is posed with the question of life after death, he sums up the problem when he says, concerning God, 'I am the God of Abraham and the God of Isaac and the God of Jacob. He is not the God of the dead but of the living' (Matthew 22 : 32). It is pointing to God through whom Abraham became what he was.

God is the God of the living and not of the dead. This is the second level at which we experience the communion of saints. This is also grounded in a deed of God. The Church is the body of Christ and God raised Jesus from the dead. In the Church there is no death. The Church is the risen body of Christ. Many of our Christians have built their lives around visiting the graveyards, but why seek we 'the living among the dead'? (Luke 24 : 5). Where we meet our dead is in the worshipping life of the congregation. They are present with us at worship. The story is told of how people were discussing the problem of Christians coming late for worship. The complaint was that they were late for the services. The retort of an orthodox priest was, 'We are always late for worship'. 'Worship began,' he said, 'with the dawn of creation and goes on. We are always late for worship.' We meet them in the church, the body of Christ. We meet them at worship, which is the living activity of the Church through the ages.

The third level of this experience is that the life after death will be a continuation of the life here on earth. When Jesus speaks of the Father's house where there are many mansions, what He is pointing to are the resting places on a journey. In the book of Revelation we read, 'Blessed indeed,' says the Spirit, 'that they may rest from their labours, for the deeds follow them' (Revelation 14:13). The best way to explain this is by another example. A person speaks of this world as the green room where the violin is being tuned so that one day the player may be ready to appear on stage with the full orchestra. Our deeds are so built into us and we have so worked here, that we are able to continue our work on the other side. The whole book of Revelation deals with the activities of those who have gone before us. One of the striking things mentioned is that there is activity in terms of prayer, worship and adoration. The prayers of the saints are purified and they are thrown back upon the earth. 'And another angel came and stood at the altar with a golden censer and he was given much incense to mingle with the prayers of all the saints from the hand of the angel before God. Then the angel took the censer and filled it with fire from the altar and threw it on earth' (Revelation 8:3–5). It is still about this world that they are at prayer.

The prayers of the saints are not only considered to be in relation to the world to come; they have also been considered as prayers of the dead on behalf of those who are still alive. There is the praying to the saints. We also meet our dead when we pray. They are in the Lord, and when the Lord comes to meet us during prayer they are there with Him. The saints are in God.

Therefore the argument is that they can hear our prayers and intercede for us. The counter argument is that if they are in God we might as well pray direct to God. Furthermore, 'We have an advocate with the Father, Jesus Christ the righteous' (1 John 2:1). The problem is the all sufficiency of Jesus' work for us on the one hand; on the other hand is the relation of Jesus' work to that of the Saints. The best way to penetrate this problem is not to think of the Saints as helping to grant our requests made to God, but rather to consider their work as preparation of our lives to receive God's gifts for us. My parents are dead. I cannot believe that they have lost interest in me. They are praying for me and much more intelligently than they used to when they were here on earth. But what they are doing is not primarily recommending my requests to God, but rather getting me ready to receive what God intends for me.

We live in an eternal present where the future and the past meet. We are going towards the promised land, but it is as promised to our father Abraham. We also live at the juncture where heaven and earth meet. Jacob sees the angel of God ascending and descending. 'How awesome is this place', exclaims Jacob. 'This is none other than the house of God and this is the gate to heaven' (Genesis 28:17). The house of God is also a present reality. The Church is where the dead and the living meet. The Psalmist writes, 'I was glad when they said to me, let us go to the house of the Lord' (Psalm 122:1). One who lives must so live that when he is called he is glad to go to the house of the Lord where he meets and experiences the fullness of the joy for which he has laboured on earth. But at the same time, God's presence is always with the living. The Church sees no death. It is Christ's body which is risen. The dead are here with us in the House of the Lord.

The forgiveness of sins

The law, when applied among men, only produces a relative standard of values. Sometimes we are more harsh with ourselves than we need to be and at other times we are more lenient with ourselves than we ought to be. The problem of Paul was the harshness of the law. He had set himself rigorous standards. The whole point of a judge and judgement is where we need not continue to carry the burden of past sins. The matter is dealt with and is over. When we were children and were caught doing something wrong by our parents they used to say, 'Go and wait in that corner, we will deal with you later'. The period of waiting was more agonising than punishment itself. The agonising period is not the fear of punishment – though this is there – but rather the consciousness that everything is not right between us and our parents because of what we have done. But they deal with us and the relationship is right again. To have God as judge is to have one who deals with us promptly and there is no agonizing period of waiting and worry. He lifts our burdens. The guilt is removed. We need no longer judge ourselves.

Forgiveness and punishment are two separate things. Forgiveness is the measure of the father's love. He never stops loving us whatever we may do against him. His love is always outgoing and is never dependent or conditioned by our response. A father does not forgive the child only after the child is punished and especially after the child has repented. True love is where the child is forgiven as soon as the offence is committed. In fact, it is not wrong to say that he is forgiven even before the offence is committed. In other words, nothing can come between a father and his love for his child. Nothing changes his relationship to his child. The father always remains the same. But that which comes between us and the father must be dealt with. The punishment may or may not take place. It is a corrective. The punishment is always within that love and is also a consequence of that love. A father was once telling me that his son was complaining that he was constantly punishing him. His reply to his son was, 'I always loved you, and will always love you, but your faults must be thrashed out of you'. As has often been said, 'God loves the sinner but hates sin'.

Above all, the judge is our father. It hurts the father to punish. We not only grieve him by sinning, but further grieve him by forcing him to punish us. Many children go off the tracks because of indulgence. It is easier to indulge than to correct. Salvation is costly. It certainly costs God. He has to judge and the judgement is costly. He judges and also carries the grief of that judgement in his own person as He sees His loved one suffer on the cross.

If we begin with the laws dealing with man, we find that we always arrive at a dead end. The law says, 'You shall not kill', but then, what about a murder? There is the whole complex of arguments for and against capital punishment. Every rule has an exception or exceptions. Today we say, 'We must not tell lies', but there again this rule is sometimes broken. During a racial riot a person runs into a house for shelter. Does it mean that you hand him over to the pursuers when they come and ask if he is there? Someone has said that we must tell the truth only to a person who has the right to the truth. Everybody need not know the truth and some want the truth only for vicious gossip. We have to begin the other way round. We have to begin with God. He only has the right to the truth. And even more, our response is based on what he has already done for us. Jesus quarrelled with the religious people of his day. What he condemned was spiritual pride. Spiritual pride was a barren product; man, having got rid of God at the centre of his life, tried to justify his own actions by various standards. Most of what the religious man does can be good in itself, but it need not lead the way to the Father. To take an example, man knows that adultery is wrong. It goes against the sanctity of the home. The laws against adultery are harsh because of this. The system of law that has set up its own machinery has its own functional justification. But while it victimizes the guilty person, it need not help to liberate that person. Society is harsh on adultery because man is so easily prone to adultery. Because adultery is a sin each man faces in his own life, in order to maintain his own integrity he is hard on those who tend to deviate from the standards that he is trying to maintain. Judgement is hard at those points at which each man has his own failings, and especially when he sees these failings in another is he hard on them, because he sees a projection of himself in that person. He basically sees his weakness in that person and is afraid that he himself could slip if he lets the other man take the road he is taking. There would be a destruction of standards which he maintains to be sacred over against his feelings which he is trying to hold in check. He rather than God becomes the standard.

To say that God has acted and redeemed is to say that each man has been lifted out of his own system of thinking and morals and placed face to face with God. It is before God that he stands or falls. On the one hand he finds the inadequacy of his own system. To stand before God is to feel the heightening of my sin, of my distance from Him. When God becomes our true standard we realize that all have sinned and fallen short of the glory of God (Romans 3:23). I cannot justify myself because I am better than the publican or because my standards are noble. To stand before God by myself is to confess to my own self inadequacy. 'Depart from me, for I am a sinful man, O Lord' (Luke 5:8) is the true confession of a religious man.

On the other hand, to stand before God is to feel release. I am no longer my own guardian. A man asked Jesus, 'Good teacher, what must I do to inherit eternal life?' (Mark 10:17). He was also one who had kept the commandments. The passage seems to turn on the curious sentence, 'And Jesus, looking upon him, loved him'. Jesus loved him and all that he needed to do was to return that love. Jesus points to the converse of this truth when he says, 'Therefore I tell you, her sins which are many are forgiven, for she loved much' (Luke 7:47).

St John puts the whole problem in a positive way when he says, 'No one born of God commits sin' (1 John 3:90). To be born again means that we are once again within the ambit of God's love and care. Our primary attitude towards God is now right and is not broken or shaken. There are still sins we commit, because of our weakness, but they are sins in a sense which will be destroyed with the destruction of our flesh at death. The act of repentance itself becomes a possibility, because we are facing God. They are not sins of open rebellion any more, but rather the result of still being caught up in this sinful creation. We fall, but get up and return to the father. We do not run away from Him, but return to Him.

The forgiveness of sins is ultimately based once again on what we do with God. The predicament of the psalmist is even more acute when he cries out, '(Even) if I make my bed in Sheol thou art there' (Psalm 13a:86). At least people thought that there was a place called Sheol, where there was no God. But now the psalmist says even in Sheol He is there. There is no place where I can hide from God. To put it sharply, it is God's presence which decides our heaven and our hell. For some to live with God is 'Heaven' but to others it is 'Hell'. He is always ready to forgive us. But the question is whether we want to live with Him.

The Resurrection of the Body

According to strict Hebrew thought there is no life after death. After death all men go to a place called Sheol. The Greek Equivalent is the place called Hades. Here it is not life, but a shadowy existence. The total mood of Hebrew life is where man is depicted as singing praises and worshipping God while he is still alive, because after death he cannot praise God nor even have the presence of God.

God in the midst of His people is only a reality before death. It is not wrong to say that after death there is no God, for the presence of God makes no difference to his state of life after death. He cannot experience God. He goes to a place which is a place of forgetfulness. His end is to be a shadow without substance, a dream without reality, an existence without life.

In Psalm 116:15, we read, 'Precious in the sight of the Lord is the death of his saints'. What that whole Psalm talks about is exactly this. God does not easily let His own die, because God wants to keep His loved ones in the land of the living. That is why the longevity of life is linked with the favour of God. To have had a long life means that he has been specially blessed by God. He does not easily let His loved ones die. Therefore Peter, making an application of Psalm 16, says at Pentecost, 'For David says concerning him, ... For thou wilt not abandon my soul to Hades, nor let thy Holy one see corruption. Thou hast made known to me the ways of life; thou wilt make me full of gladness with thy presence' (Acts 2:27, 28). To speak about the resurrection is to say in the first instance that death is not the end of man.

Even more it is to say that death is not the will of God. Paul refers to death as the last enemy which has to be destroyed (1 Corinthians 15:2b). Death is the enemy of man and God. When a person dies in his youth, often the statement is made, 'It is the will of God'. When a person dies in old age, we often say, 'Death is a merciful release'. The first statement dodges the issue and the second statement gives a false interpretation to death. The cry of Jesus, 'My God, my God, why hast thou forsaken me?' is not the cry of a man who in human terms should have thought of death as a merciful release from all the suffering and pain of the cross. It was further the cry of a man who faced despair and total annihilation. It was the cry of a man who saw God's face blotted out for evermore. To die meant to Jesus the losing of the presence of God. Therefore the cry of Jesus 'Into thy hands I commit my spirit', is already a triumphant cry over death. Death is not the last answer to human life.

But God keeps faith with His people not only in the land of the living; He is faithful to His own even after death. Therefore Peter says that God raised Him from the dead (Acts 2:24). It is not that Jesus rose from the dead. Resurrection is not a natural consequence following death. It is something that God does for us. He delivers us from the bondage of Egypt. He also delivers us from the hands of death. 'If Christ has not been raised', Paul writes 'then our preaching is in vain and your faith is in vain' (1 Corinthians 15:14). Resurrection is the last of a series of events that portrays the drama of redemption enacted by God.

To speak of the resurrection is to speak of the intervention of God at two levels. There is the personal level where each man triumphs over death by the resurrection to be, where the total creation will be liberated from death. Death is still a boundary that stands between us and those who have gone before us. We are on this side and they are on that side of death. We cannot see what is on the other side and they are also not able to have normal intercourse with us. Death is still a barrier. Resurrection in the fullest sense is when this barrier is no more. The total world itself is transformed and liberated from death. The re-creation is over with the final coming of Christ.

When we say Christ is risen from the dead we are also confessing to this reality. Death is no longer a barrier to Him. He is on both sides of death. He had fellowship with his disciples and walked the shores of Galilee as He used to do before His death. He works on both sides of death. The final coming will be the completion of the resurrection.

The Bible reckons with a time factor in the order of the resurrection in this final sense. All do not participate in the resurrection at the same time. To speak of 'Each in his own order' (1 Corinthians 15:23) means not only that it takes place in stages, but that different people participate in the resurrection at different times. In the Old Testament there is the idea that Elijah has already participated in the resurrection. In the Roman Church there is the belief that Mary the mother of our Lord has participated in the resurrection. There is the same idea attached to other persons. To these people death is no longer considered a boundary.

When we look at the physical aspect of the resurrection there are two things to be mentioned. They are in connection with the earthly body and the resurrected body. 'It is sown a physical body, it is a spiritual body' (1 Corinthians 15:44). The best way to bring out this

161

connection is by an example. We can take the life history of a butterfly. There is the caterpillar which turns into the butterfly. The caterpillar is not the butterfly, but still they are closely related. In its life cycle the caterpillar also passes through the cocoon stage. When the caterpillar is transformed into a butterfly, it throws out a refuse which is the cocoon. What is buried in the cemetry is the refuse – the cocoon – that has been thrown out of the person who has already flown as the butterfly on the other side of death. The work of the earthly body is over. We say during the commital rites, 'Earth to earth, dust to dust, ashes to ashes'. This body will decompose and return to the earth.

At the same time there is the difference between Christ's body and our body. When Christ rose from the dead there was no refuse. This is because He was not a sinner. But at the same time it is the second difference which we have to note. Those who knew Him before death did not recognize Him after the resurrection. He had to make himself known. Though he was not a sinner, still his resurrected body was different from His earthly body. Mary Magdalene mistook Him for a gardener. He walks with His disciples on the road to Emmaus, but they did not know Him. Yet it was the same Jesus. The way He says 'Mary', the inflexion of His voice and His tone make Him known. Only Jesus called her that way. He breaks bread with His disciples and they say it is the Lord. It is a transformed body, but still it is Christ once again in the flesh.

When we go on to that side of death, let those who are gone before us take the initiative. They will make themselves known. The dead know this world, but we do not yet know that world. But we shall meet, and even more than that death itself shall have an end. The Kingdom of the Father will fully come.

Everlasting Life

The forgiveness of sins has meaning only if we wish to live with God. The resurrection of the body has meaning only if we want to have the constant presence of God. In other words, the resurrection is the assurance that life does not come to an end with death and that we have the presence of God even beyond death.

But the resurrection also speaks about the nature of man itself. When we affirm the resurrection, we are pointing to two things about the nature of man. On the one hand, it affirms that the end of man is indeed death; on the other hand it denies that the end of man is death, because God has interfered. What eternal life seeks to do is to project this truth into the very midst of earthly life. The wages of sin is death, but then the will of God is life eternal. 'For God so loved the world that He gave His only Son, that whoever believes in him should not perish but have eternal life" (John 3:16). It is life now as lived in and with Christ. To speak of life everlasting means that we understand the inner connection of what God is doing to man and its relation to His presence. To turn away from God's activity is to abide in death. That is, the natural man by himself has nothing eternal in Him. There are those who speak about the immortality of the soul. What they are claiming is that there is an eternal substance in man. But according to Hebrew thought there is nothing eternal in man. Therefore there is the fear of death. Death is the total annihilation of life. The fact that life is not immortal is pointed to by the symbol of life itself which is the blood. The life in man is not the soul which is of eternal substance, but the blood which is an earthly substance subject to decomposition.

The inner connection between what God is doing to

163

man and its relationship to His presence is pointed to by the nature of the double origin of man. Man is from the dust of the earth, subject to decay. That is, he is from below. But he is also from above, since God breathes into his nostrils the breath of life. We confuse the issue when we think that God made a mortal frame from the dust and into this blew in an eternal soul. It is rather that man is fully from the earth and at the same time he is fully from above. The beasts of the field have only one origin – they are from the dust of the earth. But man is from below and he is also from above. To put this a little differently, that which is of corruptible nature is held as incorruptible as long as it yields and hands itself over to the creator who keeps this temporal substance from perishing by His constant activity over it. It is to this idea that the 'image of God' seeks to point. A mirror has value only when it is true to its nature. The very definition and quality of the mirror is dependent on its ability to throw back the image. The world is the plane of God's activity. If the mirror turns itself away from the object, it has lost its purpose and its function. If man turns himself away from God, that is the end. That is death.

To speak of everlasting life is to speak of this activity of God, when man constantly stands in the sight of God and rejoices in His presence. Sadhu Sundar Singh, speaking of heaven and hell, says that if a man loves God with the intention of getting into a place called heaven, then this love itself is not true love, but a bribe in view of heaven. If, on the other hand, he loves God because of the fear of hell, then this also is not true love. In fact, John writes, 'Perfect love casts out fear' (1 John 4:18). True love is where we love God for his own sake. It is Sadhu Sundar Singh who goes on to speak of the foolishness of man who finds it difficult on earth to spend one hour a week praising

God, but hopes to spend all eternity singing praises to the Lord. To speak of everlasting life is not to speak about immortality or anything that is eternal in man, but rather to bear witness to the effulgence of His glory that comes to rest and abides with man and in man.

Paul gives another example, when the glory of God is exchanged for other images. '... and exchanged the glory of the immortal God for images resembling mortal man and birds or animals or reptiles' (Romans 1:23). When man stops reflecting God he finds some other object which he can reflect. They are his creations and therefore mortal images. It can be an idea of himself – of what man ought to be, or some other object which gives meaning to his life. Paul goes on to say, 'Therefore God gave them up in the lusts of their hearts to impurity, to the dishonouring of their bodies among themselves' (Romans 1:24). God tries to fashion man, but when man keeps resisting Him, a point may come when God says, 'I give up'. Man prefers his mortal glory to that which the Father bestows. This perishes with death. This is why the book of Revelation speaks of the first resurrection (Revelation 20:5) as that applying to those who have already understood and want the presence of God and refuse to worship the beast. They want to live with God. For them there is no second death (Revelation 20:6). In other words, the resurrection itself is not enough. There is no point in being raised from the dead unless we want to live with God. For them there will be no death (or second death), for they will continue to be with God always. They shall be those who will participate in 'the resurrection of life' at the last day and not be among those who are raised to the 'resurrection of judgment' (cf. John 5:29). They are those who have stood the test in terms of whether they reflected God's glory or not. If we constantly reject His image, then He can only give up that piece of clay to corruption. The example that Jesus used to portray the end of man is the picture of Gehenna or the valley of Hinnom (cf. Mark 9:43). The city of Jerusalem is set on a hill. All the refuse of the city was dumped into the valley at the base of this hill and keeps piling. Gehenna is the rubbish pile. When we think of God, Jesus is asking us so to live that we will not ultimately end on the rubbish pile. All things useless to God can only be burnt. The axis of debate is not about norms and of what is right and wrong, but rather whether we are useful to God and to Christ. There are many good people and righteous people who are still useless from the point of view of the enterprise.

God's glory is the centre of concern. Christ reflected God's glory. The Holy Spirit and Christ will so re-make us that we shall also reflect and participate in the Father's glory. This reflection and participation begins here and now. We know that this is so when we participate in the Father's glory. This reflection and participation begins here and now. We know that this is so when we participate in Jesus' plans for us. Our response to His demands is central. St John points to this with a different example. 'And this is the judge-ment, that the light has come into the world, and men loved darkness rather than light because their deeds were evil' (John 3:19). Men have preferred the dark-ness rather than the light. An insect which lives in total darkness, when suddenly placed in the light cannot bear the light and rushes back into the darkness. Jesus was pointing to the presence of God by the acts that He did and it is the Holy Spirit who is at work in all men recreating the obedient man and helping man to interpret these events correctly. Man who sees the truth, but still refuses to acknowledge the truth, enters a stage of such total perversity that his darkness itself becomes his light. He cannot be forgiven, for he rejects the source of forgiveness and light.

'And this is eternal life, that they know thee, the only true God and Jesus Christ whom thou hast sent (John 17:3). Jesus is the inner connection that holds man and God together. To turn away from Him is death. Physical death just becomes the consummation and confirmation of an inner death that has already taken place. But if the inner connection has been grasped of man's life and nature in the purposes of God, then the resurrection becomes the affirmation of God's promise that we shall always have Him whom we already know in our inner life. We shall not be destroyed at death. The complementary picture in St John's Gospel is where 'the light shines in the darkness and the darkness has not overcome it' (John 1:5). It is lamplight and not sunlight. The light is tapering off into the shadows of the night. But the night cannot extinguish the light. Everybody can see and come to the light, provided they want to live in the light, bearing the shining radiance of their Father's image as they stand in His presence for evermore.

Amen

When we say the 'Amen' it is petition as well as confession. When we say the Lord's prayer, what we are expressing is that 'it should be so'. When we confess the creed, what we are saying is that 'it is so'. The general prayer of request is always answered by God in the particular. Our confession shows whether we accept this particular or not. Jesus is the Amen of God to man. He is the answer to our prayers. He is the Amen (Revelation 3:14).

The significant Christian phrase which describes God

is 'God in Christ'. In this phrase the universal and the particular are brought together in an indissoluble relationship. God is God of all. He is Father of all men. He loves all men. He cares and provides for all men. The words 'in Christ' do not narrow the scope of the word 'God'. What they do is to point to the source of our knowledge as to what God is like and to describe how God acts. It is not easy to believe that God is Father. That is, to think of Him as concerned both for the life of the whole family of man and with the joys and sorrows of each of His children. Jesus knew how difficult this belief in God as Father would prove to be, and so He set himself to convince men of it, both by teaching and example. 'No one comes to the Father except through me', were the words of Jesus.

When we look at Jesus and understand they way in which he was dealt with by God as Father and also how he responded as the Son, we also learn the way by which we can also say 'Amen' to God. Jesus is not only the Amen of God to man, he also is the 'Amen' of man to God. Even we as Christians often forget that Jesus is a pointer to the Father. His concern was to take us to the Father. 'When I was with them, I protected by the power of thy name those whom thou hast given me, and kept them safe. Not one of them is lost except the man who must be lost, for scripture has to be fulfilled' (John 17:12 N.E.B.).

We are those who belong to the Father and we are committed to the Son by Him. At baptism, it is this central truth we affirm. It is God who gives us our children. They are His. We commit the children He has given us, into Christ's hands. We cannot have Christ and enjoy Him for His own sake. As He told Mary Magdalene, He must ascend to His Father and our Father. We have Christ only as He stands alongside us and keeps pointing to the Father who is His and ours.

There is the often-made statement that Christ belongs not only to the Christians but to all men. But the counter question has also to be asked, 'Do we belong to Christ?' It is true that Christ belongs to all men, but at the same time it is false, because Christ belongs to us only in a particular way as He takes us to the Father. Sometimes we can have the Father without the Son and sometimes we can have the Son without the Father. The problem with most Christians is that they have the Son and not the Father. If we knew the Father and what He requires of us, then most of our prayers would be different from what they are. The problem with most men of other faiths is that they have the Father and not the Son, for they still do not understand what their sonship involves and what the Son teaches and requires of them. The universal is always met in the particular and the particular always serves the universal. Life has always got to be lived at the point where each particular meets the universal and also where each affirmation meets with its protest. To over simplify the problem it could be said that we could have the Father only in the way that Christ chooses to give the Father to us. This is what it means to belong to the Son. At the same time, we can have the Son only in the way the Father chooses to give Him to us. Whenever we say, 'Lord, Lord', and say that we have the Son, the question that is raised is whether 'we' are busy about the Father's Kingdom. Whenever we speak about God and the divine, the question is whether we know the Son 'who' is already busy about the Father's Kingdom.

There is God's answer to man and also man's answer to God. There is also a different dimension to life, where life by itself gives its own answer to man. When a child is born, there is speculation about its future. The child may do well in life or may not. It may be intelligent or it may not. But there is one thing that is definite about that child, and that is, that the child will die. Death is a sure answer to life. This answer has to be met.

Man, having found his new destination in God, finds the threat of death, which is the losing of God's presence, an intolerable state to face. Therefore the cry, 'O death, where is thy sting?' is a cry of victory over death itself. This new destination found in God is accomplished as the result of obedience at the point of death itself. Jesus could have served God in many ways. There was no reason for Him to die on the cross. He could have taken a different road. But His petition in the Garden of Gethsemane was answered in a particular way and He accepted that answer. He had to find His Father who was beyond death through death. Therefore God also highly exalted Him. To participate in the resurrection means in the first place to say amen to God's way for us. Then He himself justifies. Jesus did not simply die. He accomplished his death. 'I have a baptism to be baptized with; and how I am constrained until it is accomplished' (Luke 12:50). He met the answer that life has to give, and through it won the abiding presence of the Father.

Interconnected with the first understanding of death as the result of man's sin is also the understanding of death as a natural boundary of man's life. Death becomes part of the definition of mortality itself. Therefore Paul speaks of the first man who is from the dust of the earth and the second man who is from heaven (1 Corinthians 15:47). The problem of death as a limitation of man's life, as that which makes man finite, is met by the way of mysticism which transcends death. Here the Christian answer is not one of petition, but of confession. The kingdom of the Father is already in our midst (Luke 17:21). It has already been established. We do not have to wait for the Messiah and the arrival of the kingdom. He is already here. The reign of the Father has begun, for the Son rules in the name of the Father. The resurrection also has this meaning where death shall no longer be a boundary. Earth and heaven shall meet and that it has already met is our confession. The Son has already arrived to make way for the Father (1 Corinthians 15:24–28).

In Tamil the word 'Ohm' has two meanings. It simply means 'Yes'; it also represents the voice of the eternal as communicated to the sages. To have the answer of God is to meet the 'Yes' in Jesus Christ. Jesus gives life its true destiny. Death in the ultimate sense cannot rob life of its meaning. Death is already transcended, because God is already present with man. The concerns of His kingdom set the new boundaries of our life. When we take death as the last answer, then we lose sight of God in a number of ways. Human effort becomes frantic and often chaotic, because we have to wrest meaning from that which seems ultimately subject to death, and also there is the attempt to taste the fruit of our labours in our own time. We do not give time or place for God to work things out according to His will.

The Church's life is petition as well as confession. We are praying for the kingdom of the FATHER – 'Thy Kingdom Come'. At the same time we are also confessing that He has already come. The tragedy of most of our Christian congregations is that they do not say the 'Amen'. To say the 'Amen' is to participate. A prayer or confession is made, but the response of the 'Amen' is not heard. It is the mystic word. It has to be repeated by man. It is only as he says it that he learns to understand and participate in the ways of God. There are still many outside the Christian fold who are not yet present to say the 'Amen' and participate in the ways of God. There are many who are present

171

in church but are still absent in the household of God, because the 'Amen' has not become part of their life. Equally, all Christians need to attend church, because their 'Amen' has to be spoken and heard in the midst of the congregation. But we must also be aware that there are also those who have uttered the 'Amen' without consciously knowing it and whom we ourselves do not know, but whom God will justify on the last day.

When we say the 'Amen', earthly life is transcended. We are worshipping with the saints and all the hosts of heaven. At the same time heaven is in our midst, for they are already laying and preparing the way for His coming. They are also with us at worship. 'Amen' is not only part of the petition and confession, but is also the expression of liturgy. Through our liturgies, we are not only confessing and interceding, but witnessing through an enacted drama to that which is happening and shall happen. We are caught up in an eternal drama whose events are being recorded in time – petition and confession are held together.

There are three things I should like to mention at the close of this chapter. The 'Amen' is said in three distinct ways. There is the distinct call of God to which men can only respond in obedience. There was one of my friends who said, 'I feel God is calling me to the ministry, but my parents ask, "Why the ministry? You can serve God in many ways". My reply to him was, 'What God is asking for is not your service, but yourself. This is the road you must take if you are to become what He wants to make of you. He will look after your service, which is a secondary issue.'

There is the second way, when God calls for a dedication of the gifts he has given. That is when man says, 'These are the talents I have and I feel the best way I can use them for God is to become a doctor or a teacher'. But here again we have to note that the dedication of our talents and gifts stand independent of the profession or form in which we want to use them. All that we need to say is, 'Here are my talents, O Lord; take them and use them as you will'. The fact that we have these talents need not necessarily follow that the only way we can use them is by becoming a doctor.

The third area of our calling is one to discipline. The discipline of a boxer is not the same as that of a student or a wrestler. We are all Christians, but engaged in different pursuits. Even within the ordained ministry, as it were, there are a variety of ways in which this ministry can be exercised. My father once spoke to me about a letter that he had received from a fellow minister criticizing him for a lack of discipline and sacrifice in his own ministry. His reply was, 'How does he know the sacrifices I have made? His quarrel is meaningless, because he thinks that the sacrifices that need be made are all of one type and my sacrifices should be the same as his.' There was the other incident, when an Anglican priest in relation to drink had said that he did not consider drinking in moderation as wrong or as a sin, but that for him it was a sin since it was an impediment to his ministry of healing. What he was actually saying was that his obedience involved a concrete answer and anything that sought to tempt obedience was a sin.

CHAPTER SEVEN

Inspiration and Infallibility

In this chapter, the subjects dealt with are those in which clear answers cannot be given to questions raised. And yet, the subjects themselves cannot be left aside in silence nor can the questions be dodged. They belong to the central core of Christian belief.

Under the heading of 'Inspiration and Infallibility', the subject to be dealt with is the nature of the Holy Scriptures. Here again, no clear answers are possible to all the questions.

There are certain facts about the Holy Scriptures, as we have them, which are incontrovertible.

1. Both the Old Testament Scriptures and the New Testament Scriptures were selected through a long process of time out of a large amount of material. Selection was conditioned on the one hand, by common consent – those books were selected which the believing community had come to use as its main source of teaching and devotion. On the other hand, certain rules were applied by those in authority in the community to determine the nature of the selection. Thus, for instance, authorship before Ezra was a Canon of Old Testament selection, while authorship by a recognized Apostle was Canon of New Testament selection – these Canons, however, were often applied wrongly.

2. In the transmission of the texts, the normal mistakes were made which are made by copyists. Also,

transmission went hand in hand with scribal comment. Copyists sought to make the text understandable. In setting down, therefore, an accepted text, scholars had to put the movement into reverse, attempting to go behind the manuscripts to the original. It is now agreed that the scholars have succeeded in reconstructing the original text except for certain minimal problems which remain.

3. Behind the written material lies oral tradition and fragments of a written tradition. This tradition behind the text has been conditioned by many motives. There is the celebration of the heroes of the community. The saga of Samson is one example. There is the desire to give a connected narrative of what happened – the Acts of the Apostles is an example. There is the motive of polemic, such as conditions in the book of Ruth or Daniel in the Old Testament, 2 Timothy or the Book of Revelation in the New. There is the motive of Apologetic, such as conditions the structure of the gospel of St Matthew.

These motives and many like them have helped to determine the actual form of the tradition, not only of the books as such, but of each stitch in the total tapestry.

4. There is also the intention of the scriptures as a whole. They are intended to evoke faith and the consent of faith. They are not primarily concerned with imparting information. They are concerned with establishing a relationship between the reader or hearer and the subject of all scripture, God in His action. One listens to Scripture, therefore, as one listens to a symphony. The true meaning and significance of each note in each instrument lies in the whole. The Bible is not a book of science nor of history. It is like a recording of a whole musical performance. One needs to listen to the Bible as one reads its text.

5. Then there are the various literary forms which are used – poetry and drama, saga and story-cycle, myth and legend, chronicle and history, epic and apocalypse, collections of hymns and songs and dirges and proverbs, narrative and proclamation, announcement and commentary.

In a book containing so many literary forms the reader needs help in identifying the literary form, and therefore approaching it in a way consonant with that form. The kind of questions which one asks when reading poetry are quite different from what one asks when reading history. A drama needs to be read in one way and a narrative in another.

6. Not only are the literary forms different, the thought-forms are different. The books of the Bible span a very long period of time. If, as scholars say, the song of Miriam is the oldest literary piece in the Old Testament and the Book of Revelation is the latest, the period of time covered is around two thousand years. During these two thousand years, thought forms have changed with changes in beliefs about cosmogony, changes in the answers to the questions raised by theodicy, progress in moral perception and social change, the influence of different cultures with their own beliefs about angels and men, and so on. Thus is raised the inevitable question as to what constitutes content and which is form. How difficult this question is can be illustrated by using the most difficult example of all – Are the story of the empty tomb and the stories of the resurrection appearances form or content?

7. The different points made so far lie behind the problem of translation. The scriptures must be translated into the languages of the people. This is not the place to set out all the problems of the translator. It is enough to say that one has to find the best way of being accurate in translation and in communication at the

same time. Accuracy of translation is concerned with the text that is being translated. Accuracy of communication is concerned with the reader – his thought forms, his cultural idiom, his scientific outlook.

Enough has been said about the Holy Scriptures to lay bare the essential problem with which we are concerned. The problem can be posed this way. In what sense then is the Bible one book? About whom and about what is it? Is it reliable? The Bible is one book because all of it is about God in His action. It tells the story of man under that action. It authenticates itself through Jesus Christ who is the subject of the story and who is himself authenticated by the resurrection from the dead. The infallibility of the Bible is the infallibility of its testimony to God at work in Christ. When the Bible is read, therefore, as an infallible book, it must be read in terms of this testimony. It is not an infallible book in any other sense.

It is this truth which is conveyed when we speak about the inspiration of Scripture. The Scriptures have been written by men possessed by the Holy Spirit's testimony to God's action. They wrote as they knew. We understand them when the Holy Spirit enables us to hear this testimony. Experience of the infallibility of Scripture is experience of the presence of the Holy Spirit in those who wrote and those who now read.

Trinity

In talking about God, we are inevitably involved in symbolic language. Words point to realities beyond themselves. In the opening chapter of the Bible, in describing God's act of creation, God is described in three ways. It is God who is said to have created, but what God did was simply to speak the word. God said and it was so. But the object which God addressed was

177

chaos, over which brooded the Spirit of God. In other words, God is represented as belonging to both sides of the action and as the link between the two sides.

In telling the story of the new creation the same form of speech is used. The spirit of God rested on Mary. God addressed Mary. The word of God became flesh in Mary.

Again the same form of speech is used in speaking of the Christian community, the community which shares in the new creation. It is Jesus Christ Himself who is the essential reality of the new community. The Church is the body of Christ. But this reality is a reality in process. Effective agent of this process is the Holy Spirit. He indwells the Church and maintains it in mission. He brings each believer to his faith and teaches him to know God as Father, his own Father. The Father is He towards whom the Church is turned in its life, in its mission and in its hope.

Can we penetrate behind this kind of language and ask what it is that we are bidden to understand about God and about God's relationship to His whole creation and to us the children of men? The first thing we are bidden to understand is that by ourselves we are incapable of responding to God's demands on us. And yet, the possibility of such response is always there, because man is never by himself created in the image of God, he is constantly maintained in relationship to God, hence the image. The inevitable presence of God with man is the presence of the Holy Spirit. In Him is the possibility of man becoming what God intends him to be. The second thing we are bidden to understand is that man is constantly under the address of God. The determining truth is that God is turned towards man. He is constantly busy with him, with each man and all the groups of men. God is busy fashioning man. No man is a finished product. To repeat what we have said, the effective of God's address lies in the presence of God with man. It is because of this that he hears. God's address to man is in the form of word and work. There is message delivered and deed done. Man's apprehension and understanding of this word and work is always partial. But the word and work themselves address of God, we are speaking not only of some specific word and work as it is related to some particular man or group of men, we are speaking rather of all that God has said and done.

At this point emerges the significance of the particulars in the Christian faith. God's word and work is as wide as His whole creation. We can neither know it all or understand it all. However, a clue has been put into our hands. We know that it is the clue, because of Jesus Christ. By His resurrection from the dead, His life was sealed with eternity. We trace Jesus forward through the story of God in the life and witness of the Christian community. And yet this inner story is more than a clue. It is the determining part of the story, it determines the rest. It is like a strong inner current flowing within a large river. It is the magnet which determines the magnetic field within which everything in the field is kept in position and proportion.

The particularity of Jesus Christ gives to God His particular name – God – the Father of Our Lord Jesus Christ. This name supercedes the earlier particulars – the God of Abraham, of Isaac and of Jacob.

The quality of particularity attaches also to the presence and work of the Holy Spirit. Jesus is the Word of God, the Word made flesh. God's Word is as eternal as His creation. But Jesus Christ is historically pegged. The Word became flesh through a particular person, at a particular time, in a particular place. One of the coordinates of human history became part of that history. It is similarly so with the Holy Spirit. He too is as eternal as creation. He was God's presence with man throughout his story. But he too is historically pegged. He became the living reality of a particular community at a particular time in a particular place. What happened on the day of Pentecost was that the second co-ordinate of human history also became part of that history.

In setting forward, then, the Christian faith about God, we need constantly to speak in a double way. We need to speak in terms of certain particulars and yet make those particulars the means of our approach to God in His universal relationships. The particulars can never be left behind, for they are part of the universal. And yet, we must hold to the particulars only as the way and not as a goal. The Church is not the final community of God's people. The Kingdom of Jesus Christ will give place to the Kingdom of the Father The mission of the Church arises because of the particular. It is possible because of the universal.

We often speak of the doctrine of the Holy Trinity. The fact is that this is not a doctrine at all. That God is one is the postulate of faith. Its counterpart is the belief that this is a universe and not a multiverse. All things hold together. Science rests on the consequential postulate that this is a universe.

However, when we begin to ponder the primary postulate that God is one, we find ourselves inevitably and inextricably implicated in a story, a story of God's word and work which cannot be told except as we speak in a personal way, separately of God the Father, Jesus Christ and the Holy Spirit. In this way of speaking we find it possible to speak meaningfully of their relationship to one another. But then, we find ourselves brought up against the simple fact that we are talking about three when we ought to be talking about one.

The doctrine of the Trinity is the blunt assertion that the three are one. There is no answer to the question 'How'. The 'How' is what we do not understand. We do not know the nature of the Godhead. The question is sometimes asked, 'Do you believe in the doctrine of the Trinity?' That question can have only one meaning. It means, is the question of the Trinity a real question for you? Do you find yourself, on the one hand, bound by the truth that God is one, and on the other hand, led by your experience and understanding to a discovery of Jesus Christ as God, of the Holy Spirit as God and of both as pointing beyond themselves to God the Father? He for whom this question has become real is the person who believes in the doctrine of the Trinity. The Holy Trinity is the formulation of a question and not an answer.

Predestination

Among the doctrines of the Christian faith, there are those doctrines at which we arrive; they can never become premises from which we begin. The doctrine of the Trinity is one of them, the doctrine of Predestination is another. The elements which go into this doctrine can be distinguished as follows:

First of all, if God be God, then there must be a purpose in creation, a purpose to life. This purpose must include, not only the whole, but each part, man as being created in God's image and in giving to him the status of steward in God's world. The Christian faith distinguishes between the rest of nature and man. When speaking about purpose and fulfilment, we have to speak about them in relation to each man. For instance, we do not speak about them in relation to each tree. And yet, purpose includes all creation. One cannot talk about nature as simply subservient to man. It has its own integrity and man has to learn to live in harmony with it.

But since man is also husbandman and steward, nature is dependent on man for its own fulfilment. The picturesque language of St Paul is appropriate. The whole creation groans and travails because its freedom depends on men finding theirs in God.

This, however, is one part of the story. The other part of the story is this, that there is a quality of wrongness in the world which has infected everything. There is an inner tendency for man to declare himself autonomous, to deny the *Imago Dei* by exploiting it, to want to be God because he is in the image of God. How this wrongness of things and of man ever came to be is left unexplained. The negatives, however, are clear. Evil is not God's creation and therefore will be finally destroyed. It belongs to temporality. Evil, however, has its own independence, so that God has to deal with it. Evil is not just the absence of good; it is a presence, a presence which has to be conquered. And yet, the vitality of evil is the vitality of good. Evil is a parasite. The strength of evil always lies in its association with the good. Without the love of country, there will be no war. Football and football pools belong together. The desire for revenge is nurtured on the need to preserve and assert one's own dignity. These examples and more like them illustrate the point.

But what will be the result of God's conflict with evil? Will victory be won at every point or only at the last? Will all things and all men attain to God's purposes for them? Or, would God have lost in the case of some? In its answer to this question, the Christian faith seeks to hold together contradictory truths. It asserts on the one hand that damnation and lostness are real possibilities for men, but on the other hand asserts the limitless patience of God's love which never lets go. If God's patience cannot be relied on, there can be no hope. If lostness is not a real possibility, there is no problem.

A picture in which the various elements of the truth find illustration is a picture of a railway train. When a train starts from a particular station, its ultimate destination is fixed. I am thinking of an express train between two stations. Everybody on that train is bound for the same destination. The purpose of God for His creation is like that train; its destination is fixed. But more than that, everybody is on that train, everybody is going to Jesus Christ. But predestination does not mean predestiny. What happens on that journey is not fixed – those who will be my companions in the railway carriage and how they will behave, the kind of food served in the restaurant car and whether it is stale or fresh, whether the train is dirty or clean. The circumstances of life are not 'fated'. There is still one thing more to be said, for it is not enough to say that everybody is going to Jesus Christ, because Jesus Christ is the Judge. What happens at the end of the journey, He decides. To continue with the illustration of the train, there is a ticket-collector at the other end. The doctrine of predestination and the doctrine of judgement have to be held together.

The question naturally arises as to how logical contradictions can be held together. They cannot be held together in a logical way. But they can be held together in life. The truths of the faith are truths to live by. They are not parts of a philosophical system which base to be logically consistent.

Let us take the illustration of the train one step further. While everybody is on the train, everybody is not allowed to drive the train or to direct it. Engine driver and guard have to be elected. The doctrine of predestination and doctrine of election are mutually related. But the doctrine of election is fundamentally misunderstood when it is treated as a doctrine concerning salvation and not mission. The bearers of history are called and established for that purpose. Of course, to be engaged in mission is also to experience salvation. We participate in Christ's life when we work for Him. But it is not permissible to say that only those who are elected for mission are elected to salvation.

There is a further contradiction in which we are caught when we speak either of election or salvation. Scripture makes it quite clear that those whom God calls to be His servants are not called because of any worth in them. So that it is a legitimate question to ask – why are some called and not others? To this question, there is no answer. The only answer can be that everyone must make himself available to God's call. But precisely when one has said this, one has said, not only that everyone can be open to God's call, but that everyone can receive to be a bearer of history, even though it is still true that it is only some by whom the directions of history are set. The history of man is the history of man's salvation. The mission to which men are elected is to share in God's mission to redeem the world.

It is not only election, then, of which we say that it is not determined by any worth in us; the same is true of salvation. We experience growing wholeness in our lives, not because some worth in us has gained us entrance into God's life, but because God has reached out and found us and given to us the acknowledgement of having thus been found.

Faith is response to grace. But faith itself is a gift. Repentance is the way to forgiveness. But repentance itself is a gift. The pure in heart will see God. But purity itself is a gift. Men must receive what men must bring. God must enable what God demands. The doctrine of predestination is an attempt to state this mystery of election and salvation. But in so doing, it is involved in an inevitable contradiction. For though it explains what happens when there is election or salvation, it does not explain the facts of non-election and damnation. It will not do to say that when salvation is by grace, damnation is by works. But damnation cannot be by grace either. God cannot damn. You are then left with no answer to the question – why and how damnation takes place, even though you are compelled to hold that damnation is a real possibility for man.

There are those who attempt to make the doctrine of predestination answer both the positive and the negative they seek to say that it is God who damns. The result of doing this is to make the doctrine of predestination a doctrine of darkness and not of light. An arbitrariness is introduced into the character of God which makes it impossible to have Him as the subject of our faith and hope. The total relationship between God and man is de-personalized and made mechanical. This is too high a price to pay to achieve logical consistency.

Let us remember that predestination is in Christ. Nothing can happen to man which has not happened to Christ. So that even if the judgment passed on man is that he be forsaken by God, that experience of being forsaken is part of what Christ suffered on the cross. What this means for man is not easily explicable. All that we can say is that by its doctrine of predestination, the Church seeks to hold without compromise to two truths – the sovereignty of God's grace and freedom of man's will.

Freedom and Free Will

One of the constant themes in Holy Scripture is that man is bound and that God must set him free. The Old Testament covenant is based on that act of God by which Israel was set free from its bondage in Egypt. This bondage, of course, was a physical and historical bondage. Isreal was a slave people who had to be set free. But this act of release on the part of God became the symbol of every form of release. The work of God is to set free, to set free those who are physically bound – the blind must see and the lame walk; to set free those who are socially bound – the prisoner must be restored to society and the stranger taken in; to set free those who are economically bound – the hungry must be fed and the poor must have justice done to them; to set free those who are politically bound – the mighty must be cast down and those of low degree be exalted; to set free those who are spiritually bound – sinners must be forgiven and the tempted delivered from the evil one.

Unless the whole scriptural message is seen from this perspective, its meaning cannot be understood. The whole of creation and men in it stand in need of succour. How God succours them is what the story is all about.

But precisely at this point must be understood the second element in the story – the free will of man. In the very midst of his bondage, man remains free. The citadel of his self cannot be taken without his consent. He is free to choose and decide. But how can man choose the freedom that God gives without first tasting that freedom? How does man recognize that his free-will is circumscribed by bondage without first being shown that his bondage is a condition that he himself cannot escape from or overthrow? In other words,

God has to enter our lives before we give him consent so to enter. We must be set free before we ask for our freedom.

It is at this point that we discern that the definitive quality of being free is to find our true bondage. Only as we are in bondage to God does our free will function freely, so that it is implicit to speak of the freedom which God gives as awaiting men's consent.

If I should sit in front of a piano, I would be ostensibly free to play it as I like. But I would not be free as a pianist. The only way to become free as a pianist would be for me to go through the discipline of learning the rules of music, to keep my fingers supple by constant exercise, to get myself bound so completely by the musical score that I could play it with freedom. When freewill is defined in terms simply of the freedom of man to choose, man is treated as a being in himself. The fact is that he is not a being in himself. He is bound to others and to the whole of creation, and all are in relation to God. It is in relation to God that man must become free. To talk of being free in himself is irrelevant. Like the pianist, man comes to his freedom in complete bondage to God. There is a further implication in talking thus about freedom and free will. The universe is a causal universe and everything that happens is determined by antecedent causes. In many religions, this principle of causality is made to cover the cause also of every human life. Different religions do this in different ways. The most classical form is the doctrine of Karma – past lives determine future lives.

As one ponders this way of looking at life with all its attendant practices in forecasting the future through astrology and palmistry, in seeking to influence the future through the performance of vows and pilgrimages, one is compelled to concede that this may very well be a viable mode of life. The evidences concerning the truth or falsehood of this way of life are so contradictory and open to so many caveats that little is gained by discussing this way of life in terms of truth and falsehood. The Christian attitude has to be simply to grasp the good news of God's action to set men free in Christ, and then to seek to live by and within this freedom. Certainly this is not achieved once and for all. The old man and the new man exist side by side – the old man dying and the new man growing into maturity. Free will as freedom to choose continues to function, even while the freedom to choose is changed slowly into the freedom to obey. The important thing to remember therefore is this, that in order to grow in the Christian way, one should deliberately set aside the practices and beliefs which are based on one's bondage and embrace instead those practices and beliefs which belong to one's freedom.

When Jesus made known the knowledge of God as Father, the central truth of His teaching was bidding men come into the experience of freedom that belongs to children in a father's home. The problem with many is that they are constantly seeking to combine the life of bondage and the life of freedom. What they are afraid of is the lessons they may have to learn, the deprivations they may have to suffer and the disciplines they may have to undergo in order really to enter into the freedom of the sons of God. The life of the slave in the home is a comparatively easy one from this point of view. His is a regulated life. His wants are met, his duties are assigned, his punishments and rewards are understandable. No wonder when the prodigal son returned home, he asked to be taken in as a servant. It is an easier life to live. But the father's welcome includes the responsibility of sonship. They that walk by the spirit of God are sons of God. If the Son sets you free, you are free indeed.

Prayer

'I believe in prayer.' This can become a common text put above every shrine of every religion. Prayer is a common word used to describe all forms by which a connection is sought to be established between man in his human-ness and God in His sovereignty. The Almighty One is Maker of heaven and earth. The distinction between heaven and earth is the distinction between the material universe and the immaterial reality. The material is shot through with the immaterial, it being equally true that the immaterial is independent of the material. Death and mortality belongs to the material. It constitutes the boundary of the material. However, death is an equal limitation of the immaterial. For while the immaterial may not be mortal it may be so tied to the material that death constitutes for it also a dissolution.

Prayer is a description of the way in which man lives in relation to this total reality – 'Heaven and Earth'. By prayer, highways and byways are established for the travel of the human spirit within the totality of creation. Some of these highways and byways lead ultimately to Him who is the Maker of them all, while some can even be blind alleys that lead nowhere.

We have already said that God is good without discrimination, so that prayer can never be an attempt to make God good. Let us take a very simple kind of example. Suppose a Christian gets pneumonia and is taken to the hospital. He prays, his wife prays, his pastor prays, the congregation to which he belongs prays. He gets well. A Hindu gets pneumonia. He is taken to the same hospital. He prays, his wife prays, his friends pray, he also gets well. A communist gets pneumonia. He also goes to the same hospital. He does not pray and

189

nobody prays for him. He also gets well. God is good, irrespective. What then is the use of prayer? Prayer is the acknowledgement that it is God who makes well. It is thanksgiving before the gift is received. It is dedication of the gift of health when it comes. Prayer establishes and registers the relationship between the patient and his people, between the patient and his God, between the people and God and between all of them and the life which has to be lived in the world.

To come back again to the simile already used, by prayer the whole country is explored – heaven and earth – and fellowship with God established. The Buddhist does not believe in a supreme God, but he prays nevertheless to the Gods. For he believes that there is an order of beings more powerful than men whose help men can supplicate and obtain. Hindus believe in Sithi, the miraculous power of yogis and rishis. All the practices of magic that have been part of religion from earliest times postulate a relationship between the material and the immaterial which it is difficult to describe and impossible to define. Scientific research has established such a complex connection between mind and body that one is never sure how to draw the line between what is possible and what is not possible. All that the word 'miracle' conveys is that the unexpected happens. However, what is unexpected by some may be perfectly understandable by others.

The practice of prayer in this context has a quality about it which is almost like romping the countryside in search of flowers. True prayer, however, must get beyond and be distinguished from this penumbra of religion. True prayer has to be the flight of the human spirit to its home in God. Sometimes it is a reaching upward to the other, a reaching accompanied by penitence and abasement, adoration and worship. Sometimes it is a reaching inward into the citadel of oneself

190

where God is silently at work, fashioning a beauty which is His will for His child. This kind of reaching inward is often accompanied by the silence of waiting, the passivity of dedication, the openness to the voice of gentle stillness. Sometimes, it is an attempt simply to recognize and acknowledge a situation which never changes, that it is neither necessary to reach outward nor inward, because the child is in its mother's arms. And whatever the mood of the child – joy or sorrow – whatever the situation of the child – pleasure or pain – the child is yet secure in its mother's arms and surrounded by a love that understands and a patience that bears and forbears.

Prayer in this sense never remains completely alone, for neither the praying person nor God is alone – each is involved in the whole. So the prayer on man's side has its diversion of community concern which makes men pray for others. Intercession is part of the acknowledgement that I live in community and that I can never reach out to God all by myself. On God's side too, there is community concern. He gives to those who pray a vocation to fulfil, a task to perform, a mission to accomplish. God never becomes part of my private property. I never become His sole concern.

Thus, while 'I believe in prayer' can be a common text over every shrine of every religion, and the experience of prayer an experience to which all can testify, from the primitive animist to the most ascetic yogi, yet there is real difference between the religions in their essential approach to the practice of prayer itself. This is inevitable, because the religions differ in their concept of God and His relation to men.

Both the test of prayer, then, and the result of it is that men become like the God or gods to whom they pray. The image relation is what is exercised in prayer and men made in the image of God. And men made in the image of God take to themselves the image of God they create. The ultimate test of prayer does not lie in the answer to the question, 'Have my prayers been answered?' It lies in what kind of a person I have become. Those for whom magic and superstition are part of the process of prayer become themselves men enthralled by fear and willing to use other men for their own ends. Those for whom petition for the satisfaction of their own needs and ambitions is the very heart of prayer become established in their self-centredness. Those for whom the primary exercise of prayer is prayer for others become active in doing good. What is essential is that prayer must set a person free to be himself as God wants him to be. The rest must take their place in a full-orbed life. Not what I do, but what I am is what matters. It does not matter a scrap whether I succeed or fail in life's scramble for wealth, status or position, or in the renunciation of life, whether in asceticism or humanitarian service. What matters is the nature of the centre from which these things flow and to which they are related. In prayer I find myself.

Worship

The activity of worship is fundamentally a matter of faith, for worship is intended as the expression on man's side of his relation to God. First of all, there is in worship the experience of God as the other.

There is a reaching out of the creature to its Creator, of the child to its Father, of the sinner to his Saviour. And because the other does not simply remain as the other, and there is the experience of that grace and mercy by which God mingles in our lives, His presence amongst men is celebrated. In and by worship is constituted that core of experience in which God became available to man as answer to all his need. Each individual need may or may not be met. But God is known and experienced in such a way that the difficulties and disappointments of life find their true proportions.

The mutuality of the relationship between God and man also finds its true expression in worship, for worship makes man alert and alive at the frontiers of his experience. Here, more than anywhere else, man knows himself as living in God. These frontiers are never the same. At different moments of life men feel threatened differently. But the threat of death and meaninglessness, the threat of despair and anxiety is always there, somewhere. At that point worship is the way in which God is known and acknowledged.

The forms of worship have to be determined in the same way as the forms of primary experience are determined. Love is transmitted by and experienced in a kiss. The kiss is a form which is native to the experience of love. Joy and sadness find expression in song. Here again song is native to the experience. Many of the forms of worship are of this nature. The actual kind of music that is used can change with culture. But music remains a permanent ingredient of the forms of worship. It is native to worship. Since God is God and man is man, man's acknowledgement that He is in the presence of God will show itself also in tone, gesture and posture. Whether one stands or kneels or sits is of no consequence. The important issue is that posture which is adopted is recognized as worshipful.

Silence and speech, both belong to the experience of worship. Even in human relationships, communion and communications between persons often demand togetherness in silence, even as it can demand the experience of speaking and listening. The enactment of worship, however, goes beyond the question of what we have called native forms. For worship is also the action of the community. So that when we worship together, forms have to be devised which on the one hand are forms of community expression, and on the other hand are forms appropriate to the nature of worship itself. This is why in all religions community worship takes on the form of a drama. A drama provides a maximum participation of all the actors, each actor's part being held within a common story and meaning. The nature of worship as drama is betrayed when what happens is a variety entertainment. To give one kind of example – where the hymns that are sung, the prayers that are prayed, the scripture reading, the meditations, do not really support one another and belong together, one is not engaged in worship at all. The whole point of a drama is that there is a drama to be acted. It has already been written. Producer and actors interpret it, but they are bound by the drama itself. Christian worship too is of this kind. There is a permanent relation between God and His world, between God and His worshippers. The command that men do not make for themselves a graven image is a command to acknowledge God as He is. It can be most interesting and satisfying to fashion one's own Gods, the Gods that are suitable for the worship patterns that one has chosen. But such worship is make-believe. They that worship must worship in spirit and in truth.

We have already said that in worship man exercises his relationship with God and experiences the relationships which God establishes with men. Part of the consequence of this is not only to recognize that worship is a community activity, but also to recognize that each individual is himself only in community. Besides, God's action includes the whole universe and all men. Ways must be found therefore to establish the presence of the whole company of earth and heaven in every act of worship. Worship is a perennial and eternal activity of the whole of creation. It is the exercise of response to God. Every individual act of worship begins and ends

194

within this continuing act of worship which is ceaseless. In the praise and prayer, in intercession and dedication, the individual congregation must experience its belonging to the universal community – the community of creation as well as the community of faith.

To put all this in another way, the affirmation 'I believe in God' is truly made only when I worship God. It is important to stress this because there is a growing attempt to say that the only true form of worship is service: Let us love our fellow men and serve them, let us follow our Master who was a Man for others, let us invest our lives in costly obedience. This is true worship – to look after the widow and the orphan. All this is love. But what is forgotten is the interior dimension. In a family, for instance, the unity and joy of the family is not served simply by the caring which members of the family exercise towards one another. It is equally served by little gestures of affection, times spent together in happy conversation which is not business in any sense. And a whole variety of activity which cannot be characterised by the word 'service'. One cannot escape the conclusion that those who talk this language talk it simply because now the enjoyment of God for themselves has no meaning. God has become simply a dimension of human existence and God himself has got lost within His creation. The agenda in a Faith and Order discussion between the churches and communions may all sound like trivia. But they are no more trivia than the trivialities which occupy the mind of a bride when she is preparing for a wedding. The length of her veil or the colour of her bouquet may have no effect on the home that she is to set up with her bridegroom. But her wedding imposes its own priorities.

One of the true consequences of worship is that it delivers us from over-occupation with ourselves and our fellow men, and sets us free from the tensions which belong to life's concerns. It is man's end to worship God and to enjoy Him for ever.

The Church and the Churches

It is easier to define the Church than to describe it. By definition the Church is the Body of Christ, the community of those who live by their acknowledgement of Him. The definition as we have it in St Peter's epistle is that the Church is a holy nation, a royal priesthood, God's own possession. But these definitions are an attempt to say why there is a Church in the world, what God intends by the Church, what God wants the Church to be. It is possible also to affirm that these definitions of the Church tell us what God is actually doing with those who acknowledge Him in Jesus Christ. But the problem lies at both ends of the definition. On the one hand, it is not possible to point to any visible community and say, 'Here is a Church', expecting anyone to recognize in that community the Church according to its definition. What can be actually seen are the churches, congregations of Christians who in smaller or greater measure are a testimony to their faith by life and word, but who at the same time constitute quite natural human communities with their inevitable follies and weaknesses and sins. At the other end, it is not possible to identify those who in reality acknowledge God in Christ, because it is neither possible to know whether, where such acknowledgement is confessed, it is also real, nor whether, where such acknowledgement is not confessed, it may not still be present.

A description of the Church therefore is necessarily lost in ambiguity. How may we hold together then definition and description? First of all, we must refuse to deny churchliness to the Churches for any reason whatsoever. The definition must remain whatever the description, for the definition is the assertion that God is with His Church. The course of Church history is strewn with examples of Christian people seeking to create churches which come nearer in their description to the definition than the churches to which these Christians belonged. Every such attempt has had as its counterpart attempts at reform and renewal from within the churches. It is impossible to say, looking back on these events, what the Christians of those days should or should not have done. But one thing is clear. They never rejected the definition of what the Church must be. They were concerned that the description should be as near the definition as possible.

Secondly, we must learn constantly to discern the mystery of the Body of Christ in the churches. In spite of everything that can be said, it is still true that here God in Christ is acknowledged, the name of Jesus is held above every other name and the grace of the Holy Spirit is expected and received. Here the gospel is proclaimed and in spite of every weakness and faithfulness in proclamation men do actually hear the good news of God for them and are brought to faith in Him. Here through the Sacraments men do find themselves confronted by and participating in living presence. Even though the Sacraments themselves have been distorted by controversy concerning their meaning and method of celebration and have been fragmented by the fragmentation of the Church, here men and women, when they join the Church from other religious faiths, find that in spite of all similarities to the communities they have left behind a vibrancy exists which speaks of a mission and a pilgrimage. Here is a community that is actually going somewhere. It carries with it an incontrovertible testimony to the Lord of history.

To say all this does not mean that one is asked to idealise either the Church or the churches. Should one do this, one would have denied the essential mystery of the Church. To discern the mystery is to be able to see why in God's purpose there is a Church at all and to see also how this purpose is constantly being fulfilled in and through the churches.

Thirdly, there must be the firm refusal to identify any of the churches with the Church. Could this be done, then the way to the unity and catholicity of the Church would be by return of the churches to that Church where this identification takes place. But no such identification can be allowed – all have fallen short of the glory of God. The way to visible union has to be a way forward, even though viable union has to ensure continuity with the Church of the past. It must be repeated here that every attempt to make the Church more visible has necessarily to be an attempt to make it more visible in all its characteristics – holiness in living, catholicity in scope, missionary in purpose and one in its inner life of Word and Sacrament. Such visibility has always a receding horizon. There is always more than can be seen at any one time or any one place. There is a Church incognito because there is a Christ incognito.

As one can readily see, there are no clear or final answers to the questions that can be asked about the Church and the churches. And we can understand why this is so when we recognize that the Church is an interim reality anyway. When God's work of creation and salvation is complete, the consummation is described more accurately under the picture of a city than under the picture of a temple. To draw the consequence of this truth we must say that the truth about the Church has finally to be sought on its frontier where Church and World meet, where the sacred and secular impinge on one another. A frontier is truly described only when both sides of it are described – which is another way of saying that the Church cannot truly be described in itself.

*Address by Dr Ernest Payne
at the Memorial Service to
Dr D. T. Niles
held at Wesley's Chapel
City Road, London
8th September 1970*

Daniel Thambyrajah Niles

1908–1970

IN the last six or seven weeks, services of this kind have been held in many different places – in Vellore, in Colombo, in Geneva, in New York – and no doubt in other places throughout the world, for D. T. Niles was known, respected and loved in every continent. Last evening, the Methodist Church of Ceylon was holding its special Conference Remembrance Service. Now we are here, in this place rich in Methodist associations and memories, but a company representative of many different Christian traditions and many nationalities and races.

We are drawn together by a sharp sense of loss. Grief at the death of the one we all spoke of as 'D.T.' cannot but be great. But our gratitude for having known him is surely far greater.

What an engaging person he was! Slight in build, always looking and seeming younger than his years; so eager and persuasive, with his flashing eyes and rapid speech, his agile and penetrating mind, his skill in debate, his laugh, which has been described as 'falling somewhere between a chuckle and a giggle'. No one who met and heard D.T. was likely to forget him. I can still see him in my mind's eye – as no doubt others of you can – as he looked that Sunday afternoon in August, twenty-two years ago, as he went to the pulpit of the church in Amsterdam. The commanding figure of the 83-year-old John R. Mott had moved slowly down. The majestic ecumenical pioneer had spoken. The word passed to this slim white-robed son of Asia, and with that instinct for the right word on a great occasion, which rarely, if ever, deserted him, D.T. took as text Moses' question when God called him: 'Who am I, that I should go' D.T. spoke then not just for himself and for his generation, not only for the Younger Churches, but for the World Council about to be formed. Two years ago, in Uppsala, upheld by the affection gained through a life-time of Christian service, he stood in the place Martin Luther King was to have occupied. With what freshness and power he expounded the theme of the Fourth Assembly: 'Behold, I make all things new!' None would have guessed from his appearance and manner that he was then sixty.

He was, as Basil Jackson has truly said, 'uninterested in men's praise, unaffected by their blame'. In consequence, he could be awkward, obstinate, provoking. His chin showed that! But we loved him in spite of everything. And the testimony of a missionary colleague would be echoed by many others: 'One had to be one's best in such company and one's best became more than one had thought possible.'

He has been, of course, a key figure in so many of the developments in the churches and their relations with one another during the past thirty years – a leader in the Methodist Church in Ceylon – Superintendent of one of its districts, one-time Principal of the Jaffna College, President of the Church at the time of his death; for a while secretary of the Ceylon Christian Council; a patient, determined, resourceful, undaunted advocate of the Church Union scheme, though never, I understand, holding office in the Negotiating Committee; an important figure in the World's Y.M.C.A., in the World

Student Christian Federation, in the International Missionary Council from the Tambaram Conference onwards, and in the World Council of Churches – for four years the co-chairman of the Youth Department, for five years the secretary of the Department of Evangelism and, since Uppsala, one of the six Presidents; but, in addition, and not least important, the first secretary and at the time of his death the chairman of the East Asia Christian Conference, the regional organization which has begun to draw together the Christians of the great area from India to New Zealand, and has become in many ways the pattern for what is happening elsewhere. It is indeed a notable and challenging record of service which carried D.T. steadily out from his own land on to a world stage.

He had theological training at Bangalore. He was frequently in Europe and America. He gained a remarkable mastery of the English tongue and knowledge of our literature, particularly our poetry. But he remained a son of Asia, never quite at ease if he were long away from his own land. He said once that when travelling in the West and worshipping for any length of time in English or some other language, he got restless and had to go into the woods somewhere and sing some Tamil lyrics in order to recover his spiritual balance. Deeply influenced by what he had learned from Mott and from Bishop Azariah, he became the prophetic spokesman of the Younger Churches. In a sense he was the successor of Mott and Azariah, but like David, he scorned other men's armour. The weapons with which he fought were his own.

His comment on Amsterdam was characteristically vivid and searching:

'The older churches were discussing the reasons and circumstances which had let to their earlier divorce; the younger churches were only just getting married

203

and did not wish to be asked their opinion on the subjects which had led to the quarrels between the older churches.'

At a public meeting during the Lund Faith and Order Conference of 1952, he declared:
'Different parts of the world are at different moments of history. And to address the Gospel to the hour means nothing less than to live with Jesus in each country under the conditions of life in that country, there to be heard gladly, then to be turned against, to be rejected and killed, and to rise again.'

Loyal Methodist as he was, he was nervous about the world confessional bodies.
'It is my conviction, [he once said] that denominations and confessions throughout the world have a function to perform of the utmost importance ... To put a structure around any particular tradition is to make it indigestible.'

And again:
'The Church in its encounter with the world, and its service to the world, and its witness in the world, has in many places planted heavy institutions and has adopted intricate procedures of work. To put it another way, the Church has prepared for trench warfare but found itself faced with an enemy whose methods were much more flexible.'

His John R. Mott lecture on 'A Church and its "Selfhood"' became one of his most famous utterances and had a message for Christians everywhere. These were the things he stressed, sometimes embarrassing those on whom he pressed them. This was D.T. the prophet, and it should be remembered that Ceylon became a self-governing dominion within the Commonwealth in the year of Amsterdam and that his life was lived against a background of rising nationalism and a revival of Buddhism and of growing pressures against the Tamil community to which he belonged.

But more important than these opinions of his, passionately as he held them, was his concern as an evangelist. Dr Visser't Hooft, the General Secretary of the World Council of Churches, was at first somewhat concerned about the events which led to the formation of the East Asia Christian Conference. But when he came back from Prapat in 1957 he declared: 'Its motivation was wholly positive. The whole content of the discussions was the evangelistic calling of the Church in Asia.' That was D.T.'s constant aim and purpose. The Lord God had indeed given him 'the tongue of a teacher and skill to console the weary' (Isaiah 50:4, NEB). Like the one after whom he was named, he had the gift of interpretation. He was a most impressive preacher and Bible expositor, able to hold congregations in almost any land. Some of you who are here will recall the address he gave to a great crowd of Africans in the Stadium in Enugu in 1965. Others will remember Bible studies of great liveliness and insight. Many of you will have heard of 'D.T's Conferences' and have read his widely-circulated and influential book *Upon the Earth* (1962). As his colleague Lesslie Newbigin said: 'He knows what he is talking about and he has earned the right, as few men have, to be heard.'

D.T. was a fourth generation Christian. He used to tell the story of how his great-grandfather, left an orphan and seeking help, declared: 'I came looking for a shelter. I found a shell. And in that shell, I found a pearl.' D.T. had a fine family inheritence, but he knew for himself in what and in whom he believed. His was no secondhand faith. And he guarded his treasure not by burying it, but by sharing it.

One of his most effective stories – and he never minded repeating them – was of a happening at the Youth Conference in Oslo in 1947. As he and Oliver Tomkins were walking down the street, a man rushed up to them and, seizing the hand of the present Bishop of Bristol, cried: 'Brother, are you saved?' and when he got a somewhat surprised, but affirmative answer, said: 'Praise the Lord.' When, an hour or so later, they told Dr Vissert's Hooft what had happened, he said he would have answered: 'Yes, in hope.' Some time afterwards, D.T. related the incident to Pierre Maury, for whom he, like many others, had a great regard. Maury said that to the question 'Are you saved?', he would answer: 'I don't know. But one thing I know – Jesus Christ is my Saviour.' That, D.T. agreed was what he also would wish to say. Evangelism he defined as one beggar telling another where to find bread. Still later he told Karl Barth of the various answers to the question about being saved. The great Swiss theologian said that fifteen years earlier he would have replied in the same way as Vissert's Hooft and Maury; but he had come to be sure he should simply say 'Yes'. And D.T., after relating all this, would say that the question should rather be: 'Are you safe?' And to that he had no hesitation in making the simple answers 'Yes'. As he put it on another occasion, He who called me is faithful. He who began will finish. And already I know, because the Holy Spirit has taught me to say Abba – Father. '

A few years ago he sent me as a Christmas gift and greeting his pamphlet on 'The Constants of History' – a most fresh and stimulating series of studies on *Genesis*. In it he writes about 'the mood of faith' and says: 'One of the primary needs of the Church today is to re-discover this mood, not merely to rediscover our faith as such, but rediscover it in its original mood of